D0812654

# BEYOND DILEMMAS

# THE CONTRIBUTORS

HOWARD H. BRINTON, PH.D., Director of Pendle Hill, Graduate School of Religion and Social Sciences

CLARENCE M. CASE, PH.D., Professor of Sociology, University of Southern California

ROBERT H. DANN, A.M., Assistant Professor of Economics and Sociology, Oregon State College

DAVID E. HENLEY, PH.D., Professor of Economics and Sociology, Whittier College

TAKEO IWAHASHI, Kwansai University, Kobe, and Principal of the Toei Girls' English Institute, Osaka

RUFUS M. JONES, LITT.D., Professor Emeritus of Philosophy, Haverford College

S. B. LAUGHLIN, PH.D., Professor of Sociology and Anthropology, Willamette University

FREDERICK J. LIBBY, S.T.B., Secretary, National Council for the Prevention of War

ELBERT RUSSELL, PH.D., Dean of the School of Religion, Duke University

J. RUSSELL SMITH, PH.D., Professor of Economic Geography, Columbia University

DOUGLAS V. STEERE, PH.D., Associate Professor of Philosophy, Haverford College

D. ELTON TRUEBLOOD, PH.D., Professor of the Philosophy of Religion, Stanford University

WALTER C. WOODWARD, PH.D., Editor of the American Friend

## ALSO POEMS OF

WILLIAM BACON EVANS, Moorestown, N. J.

E. MERRILL ROOT, Professor of English, Earlham College

JOHN GREENLEAF WHITTIER

# BEYOND DILEMMAS

*Quakers Look at Life*

*Edited by*

S. B. LAUGHLIN, Ph.D.

PROFESSOR OF SOCIOLOGY AND ANTHROPOLOGY
WILLAMETTE UNIVERSITY
SALEM, OREGON

KENNIKAT PRESS/PORT WASHINGTON, N. Y.

BEYOND DILEMMAS

Reissued 1969 by Kennikat Press by arrangement
Library of Congress Catalog Card No: 79-86035
SBN 8046-0567-X

Manufactured by Taylor Publishing Company    Dallas, Texas

ESSAY AND GENERAL LITERATURE INDEX REPRINT SERIES

# PREFACE

BELIEVING that the Society of Friends has a message for our times, I laid this concern before some Friends. They concurred and this series of essays is the result. Of course this joint work is not the official statement of the Society of Friends, but I do believe it expresses to a great degree the mind of liberal and progressive Friends.

It is obvious to all that democracy in the world is on the defensive. Each generation must win anew its own democracy. All the facts of a swiftly changing world must be squarely faced and settled by discussion and not by violence.

The Society of Friends has made at least two unique contributions to the successive solving of the ever recurring problems of life.

In their meeting for business, where all members may take part, no motions are put and no votes are called for. Any Friend having a concern on any question informally lays it before the meeting. Friends are then encouraged to discuss the concern without being hampered by any of the usual rules of debate. If the proposition meets with favor from a substantial part of the membership, the clerk draws up a minute embodying the consensus of the best ideas presented. If necessary this minute is revised until all objections are met. No positive action is taken in the face of any considerable opposition. The final result is not a compromise of conflicting views but a synthesis of the best thought of all—a case where two and two may make five.

The Queries are another unique contribution. They are a series of questions designed to formulate attitudes of mind and codes of conduct in relation to both God and man. They are revised from time to time to meet the needs of a dynamic society. They are read frequently, but no vocal answers are expected. They are intended to search the heart and mind and are considered in silence. It is the basic assumption that there is something in every man of the spirit of truth that may be appealed to.

These methods of creative discussion in the search and acquisition of truth are recommended to the American people as a way of solving problems—they will reconcile the conflict between a tyrannical majority and a stubborn or oppressed minority.

This entire book, it is hoped, will attain the unity, completeness, and sense of fitness that is sometimes attained in a Friends Meeting for worship when a number of Friends present different aspects of truth which give a feeling of harmony, without duplication or contradiction—the final result being the stimulation of thought that leads to action and a higher plane of living—the prophetic note at its best.

*Salem, Oregon*                                    S. B. LAUGHLIN
   August, 1937

# CONTENTS

# BEYOND DILEMMAS

# I

## INTRODUCTION
### *Douglas V. Steere, Ph.D.*
Associate Professor of Philosophy, Haverford College

PUT a man in a tight place through which he cannot see his way and you compel him either to
plunge blindly and brazenly on; or to sink down,
paralyzed; or to pause to assess the present situation—to page back through his experience to see
whether he may find there some analogy or resource with which to face it—and then to move
quietly on. The inscription on a Pennsylvania sign-
board protecting a cross-road leading into a highway exemplifies this third course: Stop! Look!
Then Go!

If you place a religious group in a similar situation, it has the same alternatives. In this little book
several well-known members of the Society of
Friends have paused before what they feel to be
the spiritual, social and political dilemmas of our
day. They have searched the history and present
practice of the Society of Friends for concrete
analogy and resource. They have prepared the way
to move on.

This collection of essays is not a book of
prophecy or of proclamation; that note is not to the

fore. It would seem to be more of a work-book—a book which prepares the factual body in which prophecy may later walk the earth in daily life. Yet these writers have not been content simply to produce historical essays. The urgency of the need has pressed them beyond that. Rather they have sought through historical incident and contemporary assessment to interpret and to make available to members of the Society of Friends those features of its theory and practice which are peculiarly relevant to the present situation. They have sought to make them available also to that much wider group of seekers who are holding responsible posts on the religious and social and political frontiers of the day.

This wider group, who, although not members, are sympathetic to the Friends' approach to life, should realize that George Fox, during the early years of his preaching, had no intention of founding another Christian sect. He wanted only to quicken and to transform all those of Christian profession to the point that they should yield to, and live daily in, the power and spirit in which stood the apostles who set forth the Scriptures. He wished to draw men into a life and practice that would take them into that unity which is beyond division; for he believed that only thus could their own lives be centered and made whole—that only thus could they effectively realize among them that which Albert Schweitzer calls *reverence for life.* What Fox coveted for men was that they might "walk cheerfully over the earth answering that of God in every man."

The subsequent development of the Society, and its growth into a separate organization, seems to have been pressed upon it by the need to give relief to those sympathizers who suffered in jails because of religious persecution, to relieve their own poor, and to set up some recognizable authority to supervise marriages and burials according to a simple and unostentatious rite.

The experiences of Friends in building up a form of group expression suitable to their simple faith are most significant, for they gave to their way of life a body corporate that has borne it and kept it fresh. On the other hand, the toll which they have paid for the exclusivism of the 18th and 19th centuries, when they disowned members for marriages made outside their own membership, has not been light. All through those two centuries, they looked upon themselves as a peculiar people and tried to resist the secular pressure of life by withdrawal into themselves. Yet, even then, there were deeper members who, with John Woolman, sensed the universal note of this way of life as one able to be lived and practiced in any religious group if one would but pierce beneath the surface layers of it. "All true Christians," wrote Woolman in his *Journal,* "are of the same spirit, but their gifts are diverse, Jesus Christ appointing to each one his peculiar office agreeable to his infinite wisdom."

Rufus Jones has felt this deeper universal note in the Friends' message. In 1935 he was instrumental in establishing the Wider Quaker Fellowship in which once more, as in Fox's time, members of all Christian groups who are sympathetic to this way of life may come closer to its cultivation without relinquishing their existing ties.

From the very beginning, the Society of Friends has refused to separate the inward life which they feel quicken within themselves from life in this world. "True religion," affirmed William Penn, "does not draw men out of the world but enables them to live better in it and excites their endeavors to mend it." There is no need to wait for another dispensation. The new order is here, now. Christ is come and doth dwell in the hearts of his people. The seed of the new life is in the heart of each man and woman and child. It needs only to be tended to come alive. As they have yielded to this center and have waited on it for light and power, they have become acutely aware of the needs of their fellows and, in the same stroke, of certain incongruities in their own conduct and in that of the outer world,—incongruities which are "out of the life."

To take the life of another person, whether with the State's permission and encouragement in a time of war or by the State as a form of punishment, was to them "against the grain" that was at the heart of things, and they opposed it. Certain retail business practices, like asking more for goods than you ex-

pected to get in order to have a margin for bargaining, seemed out of keeping with plain dealings
between men. Hence, in spite of the universality
of the custom, Quaker merchants early abandoned
this practice in favor of a truthful price which they
abided by. They were not only concerned about the
adequacy of the wages of their own servants and
about the security of employment of those dependent upon them; Fox protested to a number of
assizes about the poor pay and working conditions
of servants. He even appealed to Parliament for
state aid in providing employment for men who
were out of work. Wherever he went, Fox spoke
plainly about social injustice. He believed that
these injustices were not to be charged to the will of
God, but were due to the greed and selfishness of
men. He believed that it was always possible and
practicable to correct them no matter what obstacles might be apparent to the outer eye. If he
had been told that war and slavery and underpay-
ment of help had gone on forever, Fox and the
early Friends would have replied simply that in
that case they had gone on long enough.

Fox refused to be overwhelmed by the answers
of the *practical* statesmen. He denied that what was
clearly "against the grain" was ever practical. In a
recent essay, Carl Heath has spoken of war in the
terms of these early Friends: "No one can honestly
maintain that the technique of political action that
produced the destruction of the war of 1914-18
and the equal destruction of the victory-peace of

1918 and all that has followed since is really *practical,* keeping your feet on the ground, unsentimental and free from dreaming. On the contrary, it was, from its inception, a politics that was unpractical, very much in the air in more ways than one, ultra-sentimental and full of illusionary dreams, like that horrible dream of making the world *safe for democracy.* . . .

"The fact is that shortsightedness and selfishness, the doctrine of national interests and the doctrine of security by force never were practical. The great hope of life today is that we are beginning to understand what practicality means; that is, how to practice the constructive ways of life. I am one of those who believe that the Great War never would have happened if Sir Edward Grey and Mr. Asquith and the first two statesmen in each country had been obliged by an intelligent third-alternative public opinion in Europe and America to meet around a table and discuss it first."

Yet this active emphasis upon true *practicality,* and refusal to concede to the state or to individual or corporate business, under the guise of practicality, practices which are clearly seen as destructive of the life or the spiritual health of those involved have often been torn out of their context and misunderstood. The members of the Society of Friends have been both attacked and praised as pacifists, as social reformers, as specialists in relief and rehabilitation, as practical social idealists, as doers of "good works."

They have been, and are, all of these things. But what both their critics and their champions too often overlook is that Friends are never *simply* pacifists, or relief and rehabilitation workers, or social reformers. They are seeking to live from the inside, outwards, as *whole men*. When their pacifism is real, it is only one expression of living in the power and the virtue of a life that takes away all occasion for war. When their pacifism is real, this root is tended and watered and fed by quiet worship and by continual inward yielding that restores in them the sense of oneness with their fellows and the faith in the eminent practicality of carrying this out in the life of the world. Cut off Friends' pacifism, or relief, or social reform from this root and within a generation it would cease to be a living experimental way of life and wither into just one more doctrinaire program.

This does not in any way question the basic practicality of Friends, nor does it suggest that programs are unnecessary. On the contrary, it would go as far as to suggest that this practicality can be maintained against the pseudo-practical objections of the day only as others are willing to cultivate this way of the *whole man,* of the inward life in its relationship to the outward life. Also, it would suggest nurturing and renewing this inward life by that regular practice that George Fox recommended when he said, "Be still and cool in thy own mind and spirit from thy own thoughts, and then thou wilt feel the principle of God, to turn thy mind to the Lord, from whom Life comes; whereby thou mayest receive His strength and power to allay all blusterings, storms and tempests. That is it which works up into patience, into innocency, into soberness, into stillness, into staidness, into quietness up to God with this Power." And only as this keeping close to the root is scrupulously practiced, at least by the leaders, can you keep faith in the processes of active consultation between the parties in conflict and in the emergence of creative programs that will be followed experimentally and that will themselves be open to revision when they are seen to be destructive of the life and spiritual health of the men and women affected.

The chapters on the *Quaker Method of Reaching Decisions* and *Friends and Social Thinking* bring out a temper and a mood in the Quaker approach to problems of conflict that is fully as important as any of their specific testimonies on wrongs in society. Once more, this unshakable faith in the way of vital, mutual interaction by conciliatory conference is held to be as applicable to international and interracial conflict as it is to that between workers and employer, or between man and wife. But it is not content to stop there. It would defy all fears and bring into the tense process of arriving at this joint decision a kind of patience and a quiet confidence which believes, not that there is no other way, but that there is a "third-alternative" which will annihilate neither party.

This "third-alternative" can and must be found—it alone is practicable; it will draw out what is soundest in each position and bring it into vital relation with the other; and all parties must work until it is discovered.

Yet the price of living flexibly enough to practice this experimental way is obviously high. Few really practical things that wear through time are cheap to purchase. At times, many Friends are frank enough to admit that, for them, the price is plainly just too much and that they will have to be content with the less expensive and "safer" course. Hence, the Society is made up of men and women of many different shades of conviction about political, social and economic affairs. When a Quaker meeting house is picketed because the contract for a repair job was let to a contractor who employed non-union labor, or a Quaker employer has his shop organized by an A. F. of L. team, or a Quaker school or college finds its teachers to be members of a teachers' union, the conventional role of reformer is reversed. The Society tastes what it is like to be non-violently reformed from without.

It is perfectly understandable that a conscientious Quaker employer, who has been far-sighted and generous in his treatment of his employees and has retained a close personal contact with them (going well in advance of his competitors in these matters), might be taken aback by the interference of an outside organizing committee. The threat of a less personal relationship with his own workers in the future; the knowledge of the corruption which has infected many unions; the danger of being affected by disturbances in other plants where less generous treatment is accorded—to say nothing of what may look like ingratitude on the part of his employees for his solicitude for them through all those years when labor was unprotected by organization—all these factors may temporarily obscure for him the employee's legitimate desire to bargain with him as an economic equal, to say nothing of the deeper implications for the future terms of the partnership. It may also obscure for him the value of establishing firmly and on a wide scale among employers what he has voluntarily given to the small group of his own workers.

On both sides of this present movement in industrial labor-employer relations, there is a temper to which the Society might make a contribution. In the long run, employers who genuinely believe in working out points of difference together by the conference method can only welcome an honestly chosen organization of its employees. They will welcome and encourage their workers in being concerned about the standards of other workers than themselves. They will be willing to treat with the representative of this organization of their employees in such a way as to enable the best elements in the union to assume and maintain leadership. On the workers' side, there is an almost unprecedented opportunity to convince labor of the *prac-*

*ticality* of the non-violent way of drawing attention
to its needs; and of the inner discipline and responsibility that must ultimately be the condition
of its becoming a genuine working partner in the
industry. Nowhere more than in these newly aug-
mented organizations of workers is there to be
found a group more open to sharing the message
and the experimental technique of a dynamic
peace.

The State has always been regarded by Friends
with mixed feelings, and while they have assured
it of their loyalty they have usually specified certain reservations. When a Friend fills out an application for a passport, he writes either above or in
the margin of the affirmation of his willingness to
defend the constitution the words "in so far as my
conscience will permit." Friends have not forgotten how relentlessly they had to press the State to
grant them the *Toleration Acts* of 1689 which
would protect their persons and families from imprisonment for religious conviction. Nor have they
forgotten the pressure of the State upon them in
every military emergency. This has meant that the
Quaker's consciousness of himself as a dissenter—
a protestant against the authority of the State—has
remained, and he has often disclaimed responsibility for its acts and its structure. Only one feature
has he been concerned about—that it touch him at
as few points as possible.

In order to insure his personal freedom from the
State, he found from the outset that his private

property, his house, his lands, his place of business, perhaps a sum of money in the bank as well as his respected and legitimate place in the existing un-regulated system of trade was his greatest asset. Property and the existing economic structure were for him, in other words, the bulwark of his personality against the interference of the State. "The less the government, the greater the liberty," has been his slogan. This conception has clung to Friends, who, coming from the middle classes, have usually been reasonably well-established in the existing economic order and have nearly always possessed some property.

Today the role might remain the same if this economic perquisite were assured to all. But when a man over 40, who is willing to work, stands idle with only his rights of political citizenship to protect him from encroachment by the State—even though they may protect him quite amply—he is in a poor way. As an economic citizen his rights have somehow been violated. In order to insure his rights as a person and as an economic citizen even democratic states are being compelled today to regulate industry and to redirect distribution of goods and to cut down what were formerly re-garded as political rights of freedom of action within these spheres. For private property and the unregulated economic structure have openly failed to protect from violation the personalities of a vast group of our fellows.

In this situation, Friends find themselves in a

dilemma. On the one hand, as men of business and owners of property they feel the unpleasant pressure of this control upon themselves. Feeling it in these spheres, they sense the danger of other personal liberties suffering as the State grows in power —as it must if it is to presume to regulate and control the swollen centers of economic power. On the other hand, they are sensitive to human need; and they are acutely aware of the need of a large group of their fellows whose very lives or, when not their lives, whose health and well-being depend upon the exertion of some such control.

It is not easy for Friends to revise their traditional view of government and to see in the extension of its regulatory powers at this stage a possible instrument in the service of personality—of the whole man. And yet, with the government surrounded by the vigilant surveillance and constructive criticism of those who will honestly judge the function of any institution by what it does to enhance the conditions for physical and spiritual health of human beings, many Friends are making this difficult revision. They are reassessing property rights in the face of human rights and are seeing in the government less of an enemy and more of an ally in this service.

Yet the wisest Friends are under no illusions about this neutral tool of government. Essential as it may be at this point, they see in it only an outer control. They see that the more even distribution of organized strength through the recent organization of workers and consumers is equally indispensable in maintaining any such control. They see, too, that the *real* work must go on within this structure. Within this structure, a creative and productive pattern of functioning together must be produced—one that localizes responsibility and encourages initiative.

Within this structure they recognize, as curiously enough only the Fascist governments have done (in a perverted enough way, to be sure), that the ultimate problem is even deeper than balancing economic cleavages although this is a first condition. The ultimate problem is a psychological one. At bottom it is a religious one—the growth of men and women who are becoming whole. This means the reawakening and releasing of a new community life of *whole* persons. It means the recovery of communities who believe in something and who believe in the worth of what they are doing. Wholeness is not attainable by the cultivation of any shriveling encapsulation in a theory of racial or national superiority. Nor is it attainable by force. Gerald Heard has put it well when he says that "if the State commits crimes to secure itself, its constituents will commit crimes to secure themselves. They will feel free of moral compunction and indeed will feel a very active resentment against authority's coercion. . . . The penalty of force, as of all artificial stimulants and drugs, is that the dose has to be increased until the patient dies of it."

## Introduction

Wholeness grows like a tree, from within outwards; and grows where workers and employers and neighbors and tradesmen can trust each other. This means that certain barriers must come down, and a new pattern of interdependence must be developed. Wholeness grows when a person begins to sense the beyond-that-is-within both within himself and within others; and dares to let down the barriers of fear and distrust and reach out through his life for vital creative interplay with others.

For anyone who has experienced this wholeness in the silent times when he has known the community in that which is eternal, it is never impossible to conceive what daily life might be if he were free to learn from his fellows, to work freely with them on things that mattered, to trust them, to forgive them, to enjoy them. The community then would come alive, become colorful and vital with the interplay of their differences.

This sounds like a Utopian dream. But anyone who has visited Peter Scott at work at Brynmawr in Wales; or who has visited the communities in West Virginia, Western Pennsylvania or Eastern Ohio where the *Friendly Advisers* have been at work; or the Delta Co-operative Farm in Mississippi, where the Youngs have gone to settle with Arkansas sharecropper families, will sense what can be released in other such communities that today grow-in and fester because of the barriers and the want of imaginative stimulus and of belief in something important to be done. With their families, these persons go to live in these communities and to identify their lives with these dispossessed areas. They strive to repossess these areas by arousing local latent resources through co-operatives, handicrafts, recreation, peoples' universities, encouragement of organized relationships with employers when these are present, and, most of all, by their faith in these people and in a new life of wholeness that they may discover together.

This experience of a real community has been had for the past three years in the different Work Camps which Friends have sponsored. In these, a group of thirty or forty college or preparatory school youth settle in some community and give it two-months' worth of full days of hard, manual labor to effect some needed community improvement. The manual labor has identified the young men and women with one another and with the community as nothing else could have done, or can do, and has given to both groups a new sense of comradeship and of understanding and of personal respect and validity.

Friends believe today that they have a work of supreme importance to carry out within the government and the industrial-organization pattern by revealing through these experiments the embryonic forms of that new community life which the Western world is so desperately longing for. If this can be widely shared with other groups, so much the better, for they have long ago learned the truth of the old Jesuit motto that "you can do a great deal in this world if you are not too particular who gets the credit for it."

More of its members are likely, in this generation, to begin removing these barriers by such personal and spiritual identification with dispossessed groups and races. "An Englishman," writes Horace Alexander, "like C. F. Andrews or Norman Leys who 'breaks caste' in order to identify himself with the oppressed Indian or the exploited African, does far more to advance the cause of justice in India than he could do by millions of miles of revolutionary invective. Men and women who so identify themselves with the lives of other nations that they can act as interpreters of the thought and aspirations of silent millions to their overlords are the real builders of the new community."

Yet an observer would miss the point of this service completely if he looked on their task as one of martyrdom and sacrifice. A friend of mine passed a New Jersey estate and saw the gardener working among the flowers and the master of the house looking on stiffly from the porch. "You know," he confided to me, "I couldn't help thinking that the gardener was having all the fun." These people are the social pioneers of our time; and the fresh sense of validity and of what it means to be a member of a community has given to them that sense of aliveness to a new age which they seem to possess. Something of this spirit and imaginative grasp of the transition from the established achievements of the past to these fresh experiences

27

of community that are open to us in the future must flicker into flame in the lives of those who hold the posts of responsibility in the economic and social and educational organizations of our day if they are to share in the Quaker adventure of our time. It is to the exploration of that adventure that the following essays are dedicated.

# II

## The Quaker's Conception of God

*Rufus M. Jones, Litt.D.*

Professor Emeritus of Philosophy, Haverford College

THERE is, it must be said in all frankness, no distinctly unique Quaker conception of God. The Quaker movement had its birth in an emotional burst of enthusiasm, and it swept in a large number of adherents by the power of contagion rather than as the result of a careful rational formulation of religious doctrines. The truths and principles which formed the central structure of Quaker life and thought in its creative period lay too deep for expression in words. They were woven into the tissue of the life of those men and women of the seventeenth century rather than set forth in explicit formulae. When the leaders of the movement endeavored to produce declarations of faith, they were inclined to gravitate toward words and phrases that were to be found in the creeds and declarations of other Christian peoples, and their own peculiar and unique aspects of thought failed to get adequate expression, as one sees at once, for instance, in George Fox's Letter to the Governor of Barbados. For nearly three hundred years the Society of Friends has been hesitant about formulations and never very successful in making them.

The reader who depended for his guidance on Quaker formulations of faith would wonder whether there was any unique and significant aspect of truth in the Quaker movement, and he would ask himself with surprise why the Quakers have attracted so much attention from such important writers as Coleridge and Carlyle and Emerson and William James and George Bancroft and Dean Inge. The "secret" certainly never got expression in the formulations and declarations. The central current always ran far deeper than the formulators knew how to express in their clumsy words. It is never possible to get the vitality of truth poured into an abstract phrase. It boils over and deliquesces out beyond the mold into which you try to pour it. If you hope ever to find it, you must turn away from the congealed statements and find it peering out of human faces, beating and throbbing in the active lives of men and women and incarnated in lives which translate the truths and ideals and visions into concrete expressions of life. This means, then, that if one is to find out what members of the Society of Friends have believed and now believe about what is ultimate and eternal, it must be found in their autobiographical journals and in the stuff and fiber of their lives rather than in the formal statements of faith which have from time to time been issued.

There is a signal passage in Fox's *Journal* which describes a period in his early life when he was beset with a sudden doubt of the reality of God in the universe. He was in the Vale of Beavor in Nottinghamshire. "One morning," he says, "as I was sitting by the fire, a great cloud came over me and a temptation beset me, but I sat still. And it was said [i.e., a tempting voice said within him], 'All things come by nature'; and the elements and stars came over me [i.e., passed before my mind], so that I was in a manner quite clouded with it. But as I sat still and silent, the people in the house perceived nothing. And as I sat still under it, and let it alone, a living hope arose in me and a true voice which said, 'There *is* a living God who made all things.' And immediately the cloud and temptation vanished away, and life rose over it all; my heart was glad and I praised the living God." [1] Whittier, to whom more than to any other Quaker of the nineteenth century we should turn for the expression of the Quaker's faith in the later time, put the experience of Fox into modern verse in a Poem entitled *Revelation:*

"Still, as of old, in Beavor's Vale,
    O man of God! our hope and faith
The Elements and Stars assail,
    And the awed spirit holds its breath,
    Blown over by a wind of death.

"Takes Nature thought for such as we,
    What place her human atom fills,
The weed-drift of her careless sea,
    The mist on her unheeding hills?
    What recks she of our helpless wills?

[1] *Journal* (Bi-cent. Edition, 1901), Vol. I, p. 26.

"Strange god of Force, with fear, not love,
  Its trembling worshipper! Can prayer
Reach the shut ear of Fate, or move
  Unpitying Energy to spare?
  What doth the cosmic Vastness care?

"In vain to this dread Unconcern
  For the All-Father's love we look;
In vain, in quest of it, we turn
  The storied leaves of Nature's book
  The prints her rocky tablets took."

One sees at once that both Fox in the seventeenth century and Whittier in the nineteenth turn away from the external world of Nature for answer to this quest for God, and they find the answer in the deeps of their own soul. That is a characteristic Quaker way of approach to these deepest questions of life. Except for moments of uncertainty about creative origins, as in this case of Fox in the Vale of Beavor, the Quaker problem in the earlier time has not focused on the outside world but upon the world within. This tendency to look within for the divine rather than to the sky, or to origins or to argumentative syllogisms, was as distinctively a feature of the faith of the Forerunners of Quakerism in the sixteenth century as it was of the Quakers themselves. In this tendency they stood out in striking contrast to the great Reformers of that period. The main line Reformers—Luther, Calvin and Zwingli—were fascinated by the mysteries of the Nature, Providence, Creative Purpose and Will of God. They devoted their extraordinary talents and energies of mind to the construction of vast systems of thought which seemed to them and to their generation the authentic and, as they believed, the final doctrine about God. They mined their building material mainly out of the Scriptures in which they found the Word of God for all ages. They piled text upon text, like another Pelion upon Ossa, and with remarkable ingenuity they climbed up the dizzy heights and explored the secrets of the Nature and Will of God. These simpler and humbler minded reformers of the mystical type found the complications and mazes of these logical systems an intolerable burden to their gentle spirits. They called it "a new kind of Babel-building." They declared that this entire fabric was "notional religion." The God of these systems seemed to them a far-away Being to be reached only by texts of an ancient book, or by a ladder of logic.

On the other hand these men who had largely formed their minds on the writings of the mystics no longer thought of God as a Being remote, far away, absentee, to be reached by ladders and schemes and constructed systems. He was for them Spirit kindred with their spirits, a Presence known and felt. He had always been in the world, always revealing Himself, always guiding humanity, a never-failing Light, a never-absent Word. Quakerism came to birth in an atmosphere and environment of that mystical sort. In the midst of an intense Calvinist view of God and man, culminating in the Puritan movement which won the Civil War, brought Charles I to his scaffold, wrote the

Westminster Confession, founded New England and produced *Paradise Lost* and *The Pilgrim's Progress,* this other, more mystical view of God as the Life of man's life and as Eternal Spirit revealed within man was widespread and was the intellectual climate out of which Quakerism emerged at the middle of that great century.

These small mystical sects of the Commonwealth period, from which the Quaker movement sprang forth, and finally absorbed most of the persons who had prepared the way for it, held in the main that conception of God which since the time of Coleridge, Carlyle, Emerson and Schopenhauer, we have formed the habit of calling "Divine Immanence." The early Quakers did not hold the view of immanence in a pantheistic sense, though some of the left wing groups of that period went all the way over into a crude and dangerous pantheism which seriously blurred the moral issues of life. What kept the early Quakers reasonably safe and sane and steady was their central grasp of Christ as the temporal revelation of God. They always had as firm a hold on the transcendence of God as on His immanence.

The early Quakers never had an adequate interpretation of the Christ of History. They formed their thoughts of Him primarily on the teachings of John's Gospel and thus for them He was the eternal Logos who came for a brief earthly period in human form and then, after the resurrection, became an eternal Spirit, an invisible Christ, the

Light of the World, visiting, guiding, illuminating and, as a divine presence, dwelling within the souls of men. The warm and intimate story of the synoptic Gospels did not make on their minds the same impression as did the Pauline-Johannine interpretation of Christ as the pre-existent and continuous revelation of God. Fortunately, however, the Sermon on the Mount and the social teaching of Jesus, and His healing ministry, became an inherent feature of their practical religion and gave a color to their entire sense of mission in the world.

In spite of the fact that Christ for their thought was primarily the eternal Christ rather than the historical Christ of Galilee and Judea, they nevertheless formed their thought of God essentially in terms of His life and of the New Testament revelation of Him. They passed over, speaking generally, from the thought of God as infinite Sovereign to the feeling toward Him as of one who is loving Father. Without ever using the phrase, they had in spirit and insight discovered "the Christlikeness of God." Christ was for them the personalization, the incarnation in visible form, of the God they loved and worshiped. That tender faith touched their lives often with real grace. It gave them a basic optimism and in many instances a radiance of life and beauty of character. Christ for them is an eternal manifestation of God, striking His being into bounds at a definite period of history, living a life of limitless love and forgiveness, and going the way of the Cross in unspeakable agony of suffering that He might forever show the consummate way of the spiritual life, and finally triumphing over defeat and death in a resurrection which proved Him to be a new type and order of life. He is thus the head of a new race, the first of a new series, the founder of a new kingdom, the revealer of a new way of living. The operation of His invisible eternal presence in a man makes the old life impossible and re-creates in the inner man a new spirit, a new will, a new mind and a new-natured self.

After all, where *could* God be found? There is no possibility of finding Him if He is somewhere outside of the world—beyond some far off pillars of Hercules, which mark the boundary of the visible universe. Then, He *is,* for us at least, forever an unknown God. But no more is He to be found within the visible, palpable world of space and time. No telescope discovers Him. No microscope reveals Him. No biologist's scalpel gets back to Him. No geologist's spade carries us through strata to Him. Books and systems may tell about Him, but He is not in a Book nor in a system. He is not to be found, as we have said, at the conclusion of a syllogism or at the end of any series of finite things. If He is to be found at all, He must be sought where life rises to personality. This is the first great discovery which George Fox makes, and in making it, he has discovered not a new truth about God, but a new truth about man. Here within the deeps of his own personality he finds God speaking and discovers that there is a meeting place between the human and the Divine Spirit, not alone for him as George Fox, but for man as man. Man is, thus, never completely an island, for always somewhere he touches the Divine mainland, and though finite has his linkages with the infinite.

Fox reached this discovery by the way of direct insight, or appreciation. It was for him an immediate perception, as irreducible as a perception of beauty or an emotion of love. It rested for him on what we popularly call knowledge of the heart in distinction from knowledge of the head, though this divine-human relation may be and has been proved by explicit reasoning and is held by a great group of modern philosophers.

His attempts to render an account of his principle are somewhat bungling, as for two reasons we should expect them to be. First of all, because his truth rested upon an insight, a personal appreciation, and such things are notoriously difficult to describe and to make public property; and secondly, because he was entirely untrained in the art of expressing himself, even if there had been an exact vocabulary for such inward experiences, which was far from the case. The language which Fox and the early Quakers use to convey their idea is in the main the language of Scripture, with which they were thoroughly saturated, though it must be remembered that they are telling what they themselves have found to be true, and not what they have read about.

This is their fundamental idea, that every man has—and in fact to be a man must have—direct intercourse with God. Every act of righteousness, every advance in the truth, every hunger of the heart, every pursuit of an ideal proves it, but no less does every consciousness of sin, every sense of short-coming, every act of self-condemnation prove it. The ability to appreciate the right and to know the wrong, the power to discriminate light from darkness—in short, the possibility of being anything more than a creature of sense, living in and for the moment, is due to the fact that man is more than an isolated individual. Dissatisfaction with self no less than consummate joy in the Divine presence testifies to the truth that the tides of the Infinite Life beat up into the inlets of finite consciousness. To know that there is more and to want to be more, is already to have passed the old boundaries of the imperfect self. To recognize the wrong is to be conscious, if only dimly, of the right. To want God at all implies some acquaintance with Him, for, as Pascal said, "Thou wouldst not seek Him if thou hadst not already found Him." To be a person at all means to be tangent at some point to the Infinite Life. This would be the first word in the Quaker's definition of man. Fox continually appeals to "that of God" within men. At other times he calls it indiscriminately the "Light" or the "seed" or the "root" of God within. In recounting his own spiritual experiences, he more often speaks of "the Christ within" or the Spirit operating upon him. These terms all mean one and the same thing. They mean that personality carries with it contact with God.

"Man cannot be God's outlaw if he would," for he can no more get beyond the reach of the Divine Life than matter can get beyond gravitation. Every personal life opens into God, as surely as the rays of light stretch back into a luminous body. But the will is free and this makes the whole momentous drama of life. The particle of matter cannot choose whether it will obey the tug of gravitation or not. It is irresistibly pulled. A man, however, may, as Browning says, "Feel God a moment, then ichor o'er the spot." He makes his soul sensitive or callous by his obedience or his disobedience.

He can live in the very unveiled presence of God and not know it. He may deal with the world only on its side of sense and matter, and have no more explicit consciousness of a Divine presence than the bubble has of the heaving ocean under it. But even so, God is as near him as his own faculties are, and the man may at any time turn to Him in obedience and enter into life. But the Quaker does not depend upon his own tidings of God. All the revelations of God in nature and in history help him to know the Spirit with whom he has relations. The supreme revelations in Scripture and in an Incarnation leave him with no shadow of an excuse for ignorance of God's will and nature.

Here he learns that the Being whose roots are within his own life is a Being who has always been showing Himself in the world as Light and Truth and Love, as far as the world was ready to appreciate His nature and to respond to His appeals. This gives him the positive material for interpreting the God whose Light comes directly to him, and thus the historical facts of Christianity are indispensable, for through them he can read his own personal inward experiences in the light of the gathered experience of the ages, and he can see on the world-stage the life of the Being who is now at work upon his own individual life. Every spot where God has ever revealed Himself, whether it be Bethel or Calvary; every person who has been a voice for Him, whether it be Moses or Isaiah or John, is still sacred because the same God is now seeking to make him His organ and to show Himself through him.

The most significant and transforming fact for the Quaker was just this,—that any man may become an organ of God. Saints are of no age or country. They are not limited to some favored dispensation. They do not become extinct like the forms of an earlier type of life which failed to survive. Man is not *man* until in some degree he has shown a likeness to the Type or Head of the race. To apologize for sin as though it belonged to man's nature, to assume that he is a worm of the dust and necessarily evil are contrary to the entire

idea of the Quaker. Fallen he may be, a stubborn
sinner and degraded being, but that is because he
is not what he was meant to be. His very idea of
a man is a being who bears a seed of God in himself, who may let the seed quicken within himself
until it fills his whole life, until in the power and
might of the Divine Life which has won him he
lives a free and victorious spiritual life—knowing
good and evil and preferring the good. So to live
is to be a man. It is to have discovered the Divine
resources which are for him, and to have made
them his by putting them in as warp and woof of
a human life. That it happens now and then is no
mystery to be wondered at; that it happens so seldom is the mystery, when it is the very stamp and
mark of the full man—the "divine event to which
the whole creation moves." That, I take it, is the
kernel of the Quaker idea. While that is, as I see
it, the distinctive Quaker *idea,* the interpretation
of it and the peculiar emphasis upon it have varied
from generation to generation, and there has likewise been a marked variation within the divergent
Quaker groups and branches. The strongly Evangelical Quaker groups of the last hundred years
have moved in the direction of the Calvinistic conception of God and man, and thus have looked
mainly to the Scriptural basis and to creedal formulations for their authoritative views and they
have slighted or discounted the inward, mystical
approach to God, and for the same reason they

have taken a depreciatory attitude toward man's inherent capacity for the discovery and enjoyment of God.

On the other hand, the excessively mystical tendency in the long quietistic period of Quaker history (1760-1860) greatly understressed all other pathways to the reality and character of God than the mystical one. That robust faith of the early Quakers that God and man are intimately related and akin grew thinner and less sure. The tendency of the eighteenth century to think of God as utterly transcendent, as forever beyond, unconsciously colored the Quaker's mystical approach to Him. Man, as they thought of him, had nothing of his own to bring. God is to be *waited for* and comes only on occasions as a Visitor from afar. All religious exercises, and in a peculiar sense prayer, must be specially "moved" and "divinely initiated." The mind of the individual must be "emptied," it must "bring nothing," "contribute nothing," but must "center down in abasement," "in the silence of all flesh," and "wait" for God to come and impart the word for the hour. The sense of intimacy was gone.

There was a profound sense of awe in all spiritual matters. To preach or pray was an "awful" exercise for man to engage in. It is noticeable that Friends in this period were apt to use the phrases of circumlocution for the name of God and usually names that gave a luminous effect. "The great

Author of Good," "the Mind of Truth," "the
Spring of Divine Love," "the great Parent of the
Universe," "the First Cause and Author of every
blessing," "the infinite Wisdom," "the eternal
Fountain of Goodness," "the Dweller between the
Cherubim," are some of the ways in which these
Friends of the middle time spoke of the God who
had seemed so near at hand when Quakerism was
born. John G. Whittier may be taken, I think, as
the best representative interpreter of the later
period of Quakerism in its thought of God. His
view is that of the early Friends touched and colored by the religious liberalism of the nineteenth
century. These lines are characteristic of the
Quaker poet:

> "very near about us lies
> The realm of spiritual mysteries;
> The sphere of the supernal powers
> Impinges on this world of ours." [2]

In *Miriam* he expressed the intimate divine-
human fellowship:

> "By inward sense, by outward signs,
> God's presence still the heart divines;
> Through deepest joy of Him we learn,
> In sorest grief to Him we turn,
> And reason stoops its pride to share
> The child-like instincts of a prayer."

His noblest hymns are to be found in almost every
hymnal in the English tongue, and his *Eternal
Goodness* has become one of the best-loved re-

[2] *The Meeting.*

ligious poems in our generation. After confessing
his dislike of creeds and schemes he wrote:

> "Yet, in the maddening maze of things,
>     And tossed by storm and flood,
>   To one fixed trust my spirit clings;
>     I know that God is good!"

Then come his words of robust faith and profound
trust:

> "And so beside the Silent Sea
>     I wait the muffled oar;
>   No harm from Him can come to me
>     On ocean or on shore.

> "I know not where His islands lift
>     Their fronded palms in air;
>   I only know I cannot drift
>     Beyond His love and care."

In 1884 a little anonymous volume of Essays for
the Times, entitled *A Reasonable Faith,* was published in England. We now know that it was
written by the three Friends, William Edward
Turner, Francis Firth and William Pollard. The
book was freshly written, with a modern liberal
color and it was in line with the position which
Whittier had interpreted in his poems. "We see in
Christ," they say, "as much of God as *can* be manifest in a human life." At the turn of the last century
John Wilhelm Rowntree was bringing new light
and fresh inspiration to the Society of Friends and
the posthumous volume of his *Essays and Ad-
dresses* expresses in clear and vivid style the young
Quaker leader's interpretation of the living God,
whom he had found. Edward Grubb, John Wil-

liam Graham in England and the present writer
in America have throughout the years of this century been producing a succession of books that deal
with Quaker contemporary thought, and they have
interpreted to their generation the nature and
character of God.

# III

## THE BASIS OF AUTHORITY IN RELIGION

### Elbert Russell, Ph.D.
#### Dean of the School of Religion, Duke University

### I. THE EXPERIMENTAL BASIS

QUAKERISM began in a great experience—the transforming, impelling, inward experience of its founder. Undoubtedly George Fox was helped to it by the record of the spiritual experiences of the writers and heroes of the Bible. Consciously and unconsciously he drew upon the experiences of many mystical sects of his own and earlier times. But he set out to preach only the things which he knew personally. He would take no truth at second-hand nor be satisfied with anything that he had not tried for himself. In the Ulverstone church he cried out to the priest and people: "The Scriptures, what are they but the words of prophets, of Christ and His apostles, uttered by men who enjoyed and possessed this Light which they received from the Lord? What have you to do with the words of the Scriptures unless you come to the same Spirit which gave them forth? You open the Bible and say, 'Christ saith this,' and 'the apostles say that,' but what do you say yourselves? Art thou a child of the Light? Hast thou walked in the Light?

What thou sayest concerning God, does it come to thee inwardly from Him?" He had an unconquerable aversion to a religion that consisted of mere "notions" about things not personally experienced or of historic facts that could not be made to repeat themselves in present experience.

Quakerism is thus essentially an experimental religion as distinguished from those in which speculative doctrines or historical facts are regarded as a fundamental or necessary part. The basis of Quaker convictions of truth or duty must therefore be experience rather than speculation or history. The only essential truth is that which can be put to the test of life; and the only authoritative belief is that which has been verified in personal experience or in the experience of a religious group of which the individual is a part. The reasons for this will become clearer by a consideration of the nature and basis of the various kinds of beliefs, which in Christian history have been regarded as essential parts of Christian faith.

## II. "THE LOGICAL CONCLUSION OF THE REFORMATION"

The question of the basis of authority in religion is of primary and perennial interest. The quest for it has characterized our religion from its prechristian days. In the book of Job, for example, the three friends defend the authority of the traditions of the ancients against Job and Elihu who assert that for each person and generation, "the ear tries words as the palate tastes meat."[1] From Deuteronomy onwards the growing written Torah became the final religious authority for the Jews, to which in New Testament times the oral "traditions of the elders" were added by way of interpretation and application.

The Founder of Christianity abandoned Jewish legalism, both oral and written. Jesus, Paul and John all reasserted the "right of private judgment." According to all three the Christian is free from the law in order to walk by the Spirit.[2] Christ became the final authority for Christians since He was both Lord and Master. His authority embraced both His teaching and the leading of His Spirit. Gradually this authority was attached to the written records of His teaching. It was transferred from His living Spirit in the believer to the whole gospel as transmitted and interpreted by the apostles and the church fathers. This whole "deposit" of tradition, which came to include the Old and New Testament Scriptures as well as the ecumenical creeds, was in the keeping of the church, which thus became the only authoritative teacher of it. Through the creeds, the canon law and the confessional it gave authoritative teaching as to truth and righteousness. The church, which thus became the custodian of "the faith" passed

[1] Job 8:8-10; 12:12 marg.; 15:10, 11; 32:6-10; 34:3.
[2] Matt. 5:17, 21, 28, 29; 13:52. Mk. 7:1-23; Jno. 7:24; 8:46; 16:12, 13. I Cor. 2:10-15; Gal. 5:13, 14; I Jno. 2:27; 5:10, 20.

down through the episcopal succession, had also in its keeping the means of grace and the "power of the keys." Its priests and sacraments alone gave access to the means of spiritual life, while it denied to the individual, because of human depravity due to original sin, any sufficient power to know, think or do any good thing apart from the church. Thus arose the Catholic doctrine of the ultimate and infallible authority of the Church.

The leaders of the Protestant reformation denied the exclusive and final authority of the Roman church and at first claimed an ultimate inward authority for the individual believer. At the Diet of Worms, Luther expressed this claim in historic form: "Unless I am convinced by the testimony of Scripture, or by clear reasons—for I trust neither pope nor councils alone, since it is certain that they have often erred and contradicted one another—I am constrained by the passages of Scripture which I have cited and my conscience is bound by the Word of God. I cannot and will not recant anything, since it is neither safe nor right to act against conscience." "Here I stand. I cannot do otherwise. God help me. Amen."

In taking this stand, Luther was in the line of succession of such men as Waldo, Huss, Wiclif and Savonarola, and became the spokesman for his age. The peoples of Northern Europe had been under the tutelage of the Roman church for a millennium, but were now coming of age and asserting the right to think and act in the sphere of religion and ethics according to their own sense of truth and duty.

Thus logically Protestantism was the substitution of an individual inward authority for an institutional outward one. It left no logical place for any church authority but that granted by the personal convictions and free consent of believers. This logical outcome, however, was not at once attained. The step from ecclesiastical absolutism to free individualism was too great for a single generation to take. Although the first reformers believed in justification by faith as a personal experience, in the gift of the Holy Spirit to the believer and in a limited priesthood of believers, they retained the belief in human depravity and lacked the full New Testament sense of God's immanence and of His fatherly nearness and approachableness. Consequently they retained certain priestly functions of the ministry and continued two of the seven sacraments of the medieval church, as necessary for full participation in God's grace and fellowship. For the celebration of these sacraments a church organization and ordained priesthood seemed necessary. Luther could not conceive of the full realization of personal salvation or of public worship without the Church. When, therefore, the exercise of private judgment by others seemed to involve the disintegration of the Church, as in the case of the Zwickau prophets, the Peasants' War and the Anabaptists of Münster, Luther's essentially conservative nature drew back. He dared not trust other men's reason and consciences, when sobered by responsibility and corrected by education and experience, to form the basis of a new ecclesiastical and social order. Neither he nor Calvin had sufficient faith in God's immanence in the world and in the human soul, and in the influence of the Bible to trust them to draw men freely into a working unity of religious belief and fellowship in worship and work in the absence of outward authority. Since they had rejected the authority of the Roman Church, they turned to the State for an outward authority which could assemble synods to define doctrine, prescribe forms of worship and church organization and which could also compel conformity to them. The early Lutheran and Calvinistic churches were state churches.

The same vacillation between outward and inward authority characterizes the historic attitude of the Protestant leaders toward the Bible which they accepted ultimately as the theoretic final authority. Luther, Calvin and Zwingli were quite conscious that the existing canon of Scripture had behind it the authority of the Catholic Church which they had repudiated. Consequently they could not build on the authority of Scripture until they had first re-established that authority on some other basis. Luther laid it down as his judgment that those books were authoritative which spoke of Christ. He rejected the Old Testament Apocrypha, had little regard for Esther and wished to eliminate the epistle of James. Calvin made the witness of the Spirit the evidence and proof of the authority of the biblical books. In both cases the authority of the Bible as a whole and the decision as to the books composing it were made to rest upon the judgment of the leader according to a self-chosen principle. No such liberty, however, was allowed their fellow Christians. The right of private judgment in such matters was finally denied. The outward authority of the state-church in Germany, Switzerland, Geneva, Scotland and England was substituted for that of the discarded Roman church, and conformity to the official interpretation of Bible and creed was enforced by the state.

Because of this inner inconsistency Protestantism has never been at peace. Its history is a story of oppression, persecution and religious ostracism on the one hand and of dissent, criticism, sectarianism and rebellion on the other. The gradual extrication of it from this inner contradiction is the key to modern Protestant history, the goal of which is the inward freedom of Christianity and the reconstruction of church and state as free democracies. Many movements have conspired to this result. The rationalist criticism of the eighteenth century compelled theology to justify itself before the bar of reason.[3] The philosophy of the French Revolution destroyed the claims of autocratic government to rule by divine right, independent of

[3] As in Butler's *Analogy*.

the consent of the governed. Democracy in the state stimulated the movement for democracy in the church. The era of toleration put an end to religious persecution. The Pietist, Wesleyan and "Low Church" movements appealed to personal experience in proof of the reality of religious truth rather than simply to external authority. The multiplication of religious sects promoted religious discussion. Scientific discovery enlarged the universe in time and space, so that it could no longer rest on the old dogmatic foundations. Modern philosophy tended more and more to derive both the form and content of thinking from experience; while the historical criticism of both the Bible and the creeds, and the theory of evolution liberated men's minds from the dominance of medieval dogma.

Along with these movements there has been a reconstruction of religious organizations and activities on the basis of voluntary association and co-operation; and the revision of religious beliefs on the basis of common experience and free discussion. The great interdenominational movements of the last hundred years and the movements toward church union and federation in our own day are stages in the process of the reconstruction of Protestantism upon the basis of inward authority. This process is still far from completed as is evidenced by the revival of Fundamentalism during the World War, the failure to revise the Book of Common Prayer in England, the rise of Barthianism and the fate of the Confessionalist movement in Germany. The logical implications of the Reformation were: an inward religious authority in all matters of faith and practice; God immanent in the soul, salvation without external rites or mediators; the church as a voluntary democracy, without external bond or test,—a brotherhood without limits of race, nationality, caste or sex.

Along with these major movements in Catholicism and Protestantism, based on an external authority, such as Church, Bible or state, there were rationalist and mystical religious movements relying on the inward authority of the human reason or upon the leading of the Spirit of God. Among the former were the rationalist movements which stem from medieval scholasticism and from the original Protestant position. Luther had demanded to be "convinced by plain reasoning." Calvin used his reason in the critical study of Scripture and in building his tremendous theological system. Many of the first rationalists of the Reformation period, as Socinus, for example, gave lip-service to the authority of the Bible, but insisted on the right of private interpretation in such a way as to destroy its usefulness as a common or ultimate basis of belief and practice. This was but a half-way house on the road to the pure rationalism of the seventeenth and eighteenth centuries. Chief among the groups who made reason the ultimate test of all belief were the intellectually powerful movements of English Deism, the German Illumination (Auf-

klärung), and the so-called French Infidelity.
Their effect was chiefly negative: they destroyed
the intellectual foundations of the ecclesiastical
and biblical outward authority. Deism compelled
orthodoxy to acknowledge that it must justify itself
before the bar of reason, as Bishop Butler [4] and
Paley [5] attempted to do. German rationalist philosophy and historic criticism undermined the assumptions of inherited scholasticism. French rationalism, from the Encyclopedists to Voltaire,
dissolved the structure of the old regime, which
united the Bourbon monarchy and Catholic
Church as Siamese twins, each lending the support of its authority to the claims of the other.
These rationalist movements did not control the
social and spiritual forces necessary for a reconstruction of religion; but they cleared the ground
for the positive movements of the next two centuries.

Among the mystical movements the most important were the mystical sects from the twelfth
to the seventeenth centuries. Most of the important
earlier German, Dutch and English mystics remained within the fold of the Roman church. Such
were Meister Eckhart, Thomas à Kempis, John
Tauler, the Friends of God, the Brethren of the
Common Lot, and the Oxford Platonists.

The Spiritual Reformers of the fifteenth and

[4] *The Analogy of Religion, Natural and Revealed, to the Constitution and the Course of Nature.* 1736.
[5] *Natural Theology: or Evidence of the Existence and Attributes of
the Deity Collected from the Appearances of Nature.* 180

sixteenth centuries broke with the church without joining the Protestant movement. Such were Castellio, Hans Denck, Boehme, Schwenckfeld, and the Collegianten. Many of the Lollards and Anabaptists believed in the inward authority of the Spirit, although these movements were as a whole Bible-centered. Most of them allowed a large degree of private interpretation. In England during the sixteenth and seventeenth centuries the remnants of the Lollards and the Anabaptist refugees from the continent formed a seed plot in which developed many sects, which relied on an inward authority, such as the Family of Love, the Ranters and the Seekers.

These mystical and rationalist movements realized partially the logical goals of Protestantism, although none of them achieved an enduring organization and a recognized place among the historic Christian groups, until the rise of the Society of Friends, which first embodied, in theory and partially at least in practice, the logical conclusion of the Reformation,[6] in a stable, organized religious group.

[6] See the *Constitution and Discipline of the Five Years Meeting of Friends in America*. Historical statement. See also the opinion of Prof. William James:

"The Quaker religion which he [Fox] founded is something which it is impossible to overpraise. In a day of shame, it was a religion of veracity rooted in spiritual inwardness, and a return to something more like the original gospel truth than men had ever known in England. So far as our Christian sects today are evolving into liberality, they are simply reverting in essence to the position which Fox and the early Quakers so long ago assumed."—*The Varieties of Religious Experience*, p. 7.

### III. TYPES OF AUTHORITY IN RELIGION

There are four theories of the ultimate authority in religion current in Christendom: the Catholic, the Protestant, the rationalist and the mystical. The authorities recognized by these are the church, the Bible, the reason and the Spirit. All groups in Christendom recognize all of these authorities as sources of spiritual knowledge and as channels of truth and duty; but each locates the *ultimate* authority differently. The Catholics recognize the inspiration and leading of the Spirit, the canonical authority of the Bible, and the legitimacy of reason. But the Spirit leads through the hierarchy of the Church, particularly through its councils and supremely through the pope. The Church is the final interpreter of the Scripture; it defines the limits of the canon and expounds the text. Reason can only operate legitimately within the circle allowed it by the dogmas of the Church, which must serve as the premises from which reasoning starts.

The Protestants in general have professed that the Bible is their ultimate rule of faith and practice. As Chillingworth put it, "The Bible, I say, the Bible only, is the religion of Protestants."[7] All recognize in addition that the church, the reason and the Spirit are sources of knowledge and authority.[8] By "reason" Luther meant not merely the

---

[7] *Works: Protestants Not Heretics*, 656 (1637).
[8] Cf. Briggs, *The Bible, the Church and the Reason.*

reason in the narrow rationalist sense, but the whole intellectual apprehension of truth. We have already noted how much the Protestant use of the Scriptures is dependent upon reason; and how much the Reformers relied upon the leading of the Spirit in the individual soul. Practically all the Protestant sects have given the Church a large authority in discipline and doctrine. They have frequently used an enfeebled power of excommunication and invoked the power of the State when they could in order to standardize the interpretation of the Scriptures. In reality the Bible has never been to the Protestant believer the ultimate authority, except in theory. Luther, Calvin and Zwingli all denied to others that right of private judgment which they claimed for themselves; and their successors have walked in their ways.

Reason is for the rationalists, such as the English Deists and the devotees of the continental *Illumination,* the supreme authority. They granted to all men without grudging the right of appeal to reason which Luther claimed for himself; and they did full justice to the Protestant appeal, acknowledged or unacknowledged, to processes of reasoning in proving the canon, in establishing the text and in translating and interpreting the Scriptures. The rationalists, nevertheless, used reason in the restricted sense of formal logical reasoning; according to which, one can only get in the conclusion what is actually implicit in the premises. The premises may consist of axioms as in the case of mathematical reasoning; or of the dogmas of the Church, as with medieval scholasticism; or of beliefs generally accepted because they are in agreement with the customs, general experiences, or beliefs of an age. For example, English Deism, for the most part, started with the assumption that "natural religion" was to be accepted as the norm of what was reasonable to believe. Their age actually knew little of primitive or uncorrupted religion; but they assumed that the only reasonable beliefs were the existence of God, the immortality of the soul, and the moral law.

Reason as thus defined is an inward authority, but one of limited validity. The chief value of it is (1) as a critic of accepted premises and assumptions, which no longer correspond with the common experience of mankind, or which changed circumstances have rendered invalid; and (2) as a guide to new facts and experiences through the formulation and examination of working hypotheses (doctrines, in theology). It can deal well only with matters that can be expressed in precise formulas or are capable of exact definition. There is a wide range or religious experience and of religious values which cannot be reached by this kind of reasoning.

The mystics put the final source of authority wholly within the individual. It is here in the inner shrine of the soul that the mystic meets with God and learns of his character and will. The leading of the Spirit, to be sure, is common ground of all Christian sects; but with the Catholics the working of the Spirit is chiefly limited to the leadership of the Church; and among Protestant sects, primarily to the inspiration of the Scriptures. The individual in these communions is not to follow his leadings as to truth and right except within the limits and under the censorship of the Scripture or of tradition as interpreted by an external authority.

For the mystic, on the contrary, the ultimate spiritual authority must be the personal conviction of truth and righteousness. To this many things may contribute: the experience of others, whose spiritual wisdom is esteemed; the voice of the Church; the teaching of Scripture; the reasonableness of a belief in the light of all known truth. Yet none of them can be valid against the final inward conviction of reality and duty.

This inward authorization is actually the decisive element even in the case of those who acknowledge outward authorities. One may not yield obedience to the Church unless he is convinced that the Church has a right to his obedience.[9] One may not accept the Scriptures as the ultimate rule of faith and practice in things moral and spiritual until he has become convinced—by church authority, reason or experience, or by all three—that these books as composed, collected, translated, transmit-

[9] John Henry Newman thought to restrict the right of private judgment to the choice of a competent teacher. *Essays, Critical and Historical.* No. XIV (ca. 1845).

ted and interpreted are the very word of God. One may not follow his own reason, if he believe it to be incompetent through human depravity, nor even follow the leading of the Spirit in his own soul until convinced that it is the leading of *God's* Spirit and not an evil spirit and that he rightly apprehends it.

The crux of the matter is that in religions of authority, theoretically at least, in cases where the inward and outward authorities clash, as when Luther's conscience revolted at Tetzel's sale of indulgences, the individual is required to accept as true what seems to him false; to obey, even against conscience, and call it virtue; to do as right what is believed to be wrong.

On the other hand, the inward authority cannot be accepted as infallible. For the rationalist and mystic it must be final, but it cannot be infallible. Our human means of attaining the knowledge of things spiritual are subject to the finite liability to error which affects our sense-perceptions. In neither the material nor spiritual realm is infallibility granted us. However, just as our senses, if critically used, are sufficient for the practical purposes of life, so is our spiritual apprehension.


## IV. CONSCIENCE

The relation of conscience to the Inner Light is important. The two are not identical, although they are closely related. As the reason is one of the "organs" of the Inner Light, the organ of intellectual or logical apprehension, so conscience is its organ of moral judgment. It speaks, not as an outward or external judge or authority, but as the soul's supreme tribunal, passing judgment on all proposed or contemplated acts. The soul can have no appeal from its judgments, for it cannot appeal from itself. It is for the soul an ultimate tribunal and thus speaks as God.[10] The conscience is primarily a judge of motives, and here its judgment is infallible as well as final. It approves, if we intend to do right, and condemns, if we believe our conduct to be wrong.

There is also another element in conscience, which is variable and fallible. Our motives are based on our beliefs as to the nature and effect of our acts. Here we are at the mercy of custom, education, prejudice and limited knowledge. These judgments as to the right and wrong nature of conduct may vary with the individual and change with growing knowledge and widening experience or greater social sensitiveness. These changing ideas as to the nature and effects of conduct will be reflected in the judgments of conscience. In this respect, conscience is particularly in jeopardy of becoming the victim of rationalization, of self-interest, of custom, of institutional bias. Because of this the consciences of men are not uniform nor are they infallible guides as to the details of conduct. They are subject to correction. If a man be sinning

[10] I John 3:19-22.

against conscience, he needs to be converted, so that henceforth he will heed it. If he be conscientiously engaged in practices that are harmful to himself and his neighbors, he needs to be enlightened as to the true nature of his acts. It follows that a man may be a great sinner against his fellowmen, while having a good conscience toward God. To be conscientious is inescapably obligatory, but conscientiousness is not enough; one must also be intelligent.[11] Conscience then is an organ of the Inner Light, but it falls short of giving the full knowledge of God; more is required for that than sincerity; it requires righteousness, mercy, love and peace. "Though we cannot make the immense assertion that conscience is absolutely infallible and a precise guide under any and every circumstance of life, it is nevertheless the surest moral authority within our reach,—a voice to be implicitly obeyed in the crisis of an action. It is our highest guide. No command on earth can take precedence of it. Nothing more autonomous or more worthy of obedience can be discovered."[12]

### V. THE INNER LIGHT

The Quaker idea of the inward authority in religion has been expressed in many ways. It has been called the Inner Light, the Christ within, the

[11] Blanshard, B., *Inward Light and Outward Darkness*. Pamphlet published by Friends General Conference. Philadelphia.
[12] Jones, Rufus M., *The Nature and Authority of Conscience*, p. 72.

spirit of Christ, the Seed, the Seed of God, and that of God in men, beside many purely biblical expressions, such as Christ, the Spirit of God, the Holy Spirit, etc.

Friends have never developed an official system of theology and have not felt the necessity of exact theological terminology. In early Friends' usage the expression the "Inner Light" was never precisely defined. It is fairly clear that it was used to express at least three concepts, closely related in experience but logically distinct: (1) God as known to the individual directly and inwardly. This assumes the divine immanence. (2) Human capacity for spiritual knowledge. This differs from the Calvinistic conception of grace as the bestowal upon the elect of a capacity which man does not "naturally" have, due to his depraved nature. (3) The character, will and power of God as thus known in personal experience.

Robert Barclay was our most systematic thinker. Brought up in Scotland and educated by the Catholics, he retained a theoretic belief in human depravity. He distinguished between human nature as such and human nature as it was rendered spiritually capable through the gift of the Inner Light to every man coming into the world. The practical difference, which this conception of the Inner Light as an addendum to man's natural capacities makes, would seem slight, since on either view every man has the Light. Nevertheless it did tend to disparage the ordinary processes of knowledge as belonging to the "depraved" part of man's equipment. It preserved a theoretical natural dichotomy in man, which afforded lodgement to the Quietist fear of "creaturely activity" and the Evangelical depreciation of "mere morality" and the human reason. It prepared the way for the great change in emphasis which the Evangelical influence made in English and American Quakerism in the nineteenth century, while it obscured the fact that a change had taken place. It tended to regard spiritual guidance as an abnormal procedure, and exalted the importance of unusual psychical states and of rare experiences.

Most of the early Quaker leaders believed that the Inner Light is part of man's native endowment, in which he is conjunct with God and by which God may be known, apprehended and acknowledged. Reason and conscience are part of its equipment. It includes all the means by which man may apprehend truth, beauty, and righteousness.

The Inner Light never meant for Friends any inevitable or necessary goodness, or intellectual or spiritual infallibility; although as representing the divine light or voice, it was regarded by early Friends frequently as infallible. Friends arose in an age that felt keenly a need for an infallibility to match the claimed infallibilties of church, Bible or reason. Isaac Penington says that "the Light is an infallible light, and the eye that sees it, is an infallible eye." But Friends were quite conscious of the danger (especially in others) that the eye might not see clearly; for, to use Paul's figure, "we have this treasure in earthen vessels." The "Seed" stood for certain spiritual capacities and opportunities—for potentialities of divine sonship, which must be realized by constant dedication and spiritual discipline.

The sacramental system of historic Christianity is built upon the conception of man's depravity and God's aloofness, so that only by supernatural endowment, special revelation and the divine presence uniquely manifest in sacramental objects can the gap be bridged. The Quaker view of authority removes the fundamental presuppositions of this theory; but outward means of spiritual knowledge and experience are not thereby rendered useless, even though they are not essential. Not all persons are equal in spiritual capacity and discernment. Aids to the clearer knowledge of God are needed. Just as tea tasters need to improve their natural sensory capacity by careful use, and musicians must cultivate their natural gifts by study and practice, so spiritual discernment improves with attention and use. Worship, education, seeking, meditation and study—all these are invaluable in the making of the Inner Light more efficient. The Inner Light is independent of any outward form or observance. The knowledge of God, of His will and truth, is not conditioned on any specific rite, ceremony, or object. Nevertheless it may be strengthened and clarified by spiritual exercises and disciplines.

These are to be judged by their fruits, by their efficacy in clarifying the spiritual vision and strengthening the devotion to duty. In mystical experience each person or group must find its own best way to the knowledge of God.

Among Friends private devotions, especially the receptive "waiting on God"; the devotional use of the Bible, as the end to which all critical, historical and literary studies lead; group worship, especially of the seeking, informal, "sharing" types; and the use of religious literature and church history in general have all been found valuable.

The Inner Light as an ultimate authority is not to be confused with its psychological mechanisms or with epistemological theories as to its origin and processes. The vital question is whether reality is revealed. Discussion of psychological processes is valuable, if it help clarify beliefs or perfect the soul's technique. Truth may come to the human mind in many ways. God has left himself a thousand doors through which He may make himself known to the human soul; but not all processes of spiritual knowledge are equally reliable or rewarding. All need to be used with religious seriousness and critical care. But the Inner Light is neither to be identified with the logical reason nor denied use of it; it uses conscience but surpasses it; it is not identical with intuition or the subconscious; it is not shut up to psychopathic or abnormal states nor to instinctive urges. Just as the human spirit is equipped to reach reality through

67

sense impressions, it has the ability to discern truth and right in the spiritual world. As it is able to recognize other personalities when brought into contact with them, so it can sense the presence of God and come into fellowship with him.

In the outer or material world, knowledge is mediated by sense impressions; but the mind must interpret them and subject them to criticism before it gets reality from them. One may not believe his eyes always. Other senses must be used to check what the eyes report. Past experiences must be called in through memory to check the present report of the senses. Reason must compare, interpret, and sit in judgment; emotion and will must evaluate—all this before the mind recognizes as truth what the senses give. In the last analysis, however, we live by the conviction that the senses do bring us knowledge of objective reality, of which groups of men may have common knowledge. This knowledge is sufficiently exact, even though not infallible, to serve as a practicable basis of both personal and social life.

In like manner spiritual things are spiritually discerned. To follow "the mystic way" is the greatest adventure of the human spirit. The Christian spirit must distinguish true from false in its psychic and phenomenal endowment. The psychic self is such a strange mixture of good and evil, of truth and error, of primitive urges and passions, of selfish desires and altruistic impulses, that it is difficult to know and follow the voice of God amid

the inner confusion; to distinguish the impulses of
the flesh from the movings of the Spirit. The Inner
Light must be attended diligently, the powers of
spiritual vision carefully cultivated, and the inner
leading sifted critically, if the inward authority
is to be a true guide. The dream must be distinguished from the word of God, and instinctive
urges winnowed out from the strong movings of
God's Spirit within. Personal desires must not be
taken as the voice of God. The stamp of supreme
reality and authority must be set on righteousness,
mercy, justice, love and self-sacrifice. The divine
hierarchy of values must be established and kept
intact when lesser goods try to sit in the seat of the
Supreme Good. One must learn not to mistake "for
the all-perfect good Thou art, some grim creation
of his heart."

The end of all knowing processes is the consciousness of reality. Conviction, belief, and knowledge are final acts of the human personality as a
knowing or cognitive being. They presuppose a
capacity to recognize reality when clearly presented, each form through its appropriate channel.
The soul has its own capacity to know God, just
as it has a capacity to recognize beauty or truth,
and to respond to manifestations of Himself. Beyond this we may not go.

In these experiences one comes to know God,
and to make Him the judge of all claims to goodness and truth. We may know God as surely as we
know the world of sense, although by different

means. For there is a distinguishable spiritual reality here, objective enough to form the basis of common belief and experience, usable by all sorts and conditions of men, practical as the basis of human social as well as individual conduct.

Outward authorities may and do contribute to one's sense of reality. Public worship with its sharing and stimulus; the Scriptures with their treasure of wisdom and experience, and their examples of saintly character; the voice of tradition, custom, public opinion, great leaders, great hoary institutions like Church and State—all these command attention and must be weighed in "making up the main account" with truth and duty. Yet none of these can bind the soul, if and when it judges that what they offer is untruth or unrighteousness and so not of God. The soul is never under obligation to pretend to accept as true what it finally believes to be false; nor to accept as a moral obligation the suggestion or command to do what it is convinced is wrong.

A man may find himself unable to decide a question which involves facts and fields beyond his experience or competence. In such cases he may take the word of experts or accept the authority of institutions as the basis of his own beliefs or conduct; but in such cases the decision to trust and the conviction that the "authority" is trustworthy are his own; and he can follow its counsel or direction only so long as his faith in its competence in general remains, or its particular injunctions do not contradict his own particular convictions of right. Luther believed in the Church until it supported Tetzel's sale of indulgences, which so outraged Luther's sense of right that no outward authority could justify it to him. Augustine of Hippo believed Manichaeus when he claimed to be an incarnation of the Holy Spirit with virtual omniscience until his statements about the eclipses of sun and moon contradicted Augustine's verified knowledge about them. After that he could no longer follow Manichaeus as a spiritual authority.

The "Inner Light" is thus an ultimate authority within the soul. It cannot be referred to something beyond, to a more august authority. Whatever its relation to other factors of the psychic self, however related to other psychological processes and influenced by external factors, it is still the soul's ultimate power of decision as to truth, right and duty. The reason, the esthetic sense, the conscience —these are the soul's ultimate tribunals as to truth, beauty and right. There is no appeal for the individual from their findings. What they say is true, beautiful and right are inescapably true, beautiful and right for that person. In the same way the will is autonomous. No other will can take the place of it; and the person himself, although he can change his decision, cannot substitute another's will or act by it. For the will is the final set of all the personal powers toward an act or a course of conduct. The Inner Light is also one of the ultimates of the soul. It speaks for God and the soul, in the soul with a voice of ultimate authority as synthesis of all personal judgments of truth, beauty and duty in a sense of cosmic reality and obligation. Thus it is, and only thus is it, a valid and final authority.

The final test of its validity as a guide and sponsor for the individual in his social relations must be the empirical test of experience. How does the Inner Light work as an ultimate authority? How does it compare with the results attained by those who accept Church and State as final authorities? Can it produce balanced, unified, efficient personalities? In practice can it escape the dangers of unregulated individualism, or irrational subjectivity? Does it seem to have an objective basis in spiritual reality, so that rightly used it can produce common ideals and working beliefs? Can it produce a type of character that is socially competent?

Judgment on these points must be relative. No authority has ever provided for the common welfare perfectly. Any authority must be acknowledged and generally obeyed if it is to serve satisfactorily as a basis of society. By outward compulsion an institution can secure a fair degree of social conformity as long as it is accepted voluntarily by a large majority as in totalitarian states today. An inward authority cannot maintain such a specious appearance of unanimity. It can only secure the co-operation of those who do so from inward impulsion. It must use the method of "convincement" to get conformity.

The answer to these questions must be sought in

the experience of the Christian mystics of many ages; and particularly of the many brotherhood groups who have been able to live holy and socially constructive lives by the inward authority. The Quaker experience may be cited in corroboration. The Society of Friends has been made up of men of like passions with the rest of humanity,—subject to the same impulses of the flesh, the same proneness to error in judgment, the same frailties of spirit.

In spite of the shortcomings of individuals and groups the Society has maintained a high average of Christian character. The Quaker has become proverbial for spiritual poise and moral force. He would not run with the multitude to do evil. He has cherished a catholic ideal of human brotherhood. The Society has been a nursery of spiritually sensitive souls, with keen prevision of moral issues and practical sympathy with all suffering. It has produced pioneer leaders in a surprising number of philanthropic and religious movements. The Quaker has been in general as willing to sacrifice and suffer for high ideals of human weal as he has been unwilling to inflict suffering on others. If the Quaker experience is in any adequate measure a test, the Inner Light is a practicable basis of human society.

Authoritative creeds and disciplines are usually regarded as socially useful and even necessary, because they provide a basis for social unity and co-operation. In the experience of Friends, the Inner

Light has proven capable of securing sufficient agreement in doctrinal beliefs and standards of character and in social ideals to form the basis of a stable society.

The Inner Light affords access to objective spiritual realities. The pure in heart see God. They that seek Him find Him. The inward authority is not pure subjectivism; it does not mean a religious and moral anarchy, where each individual is "a church by himself."

The natural sciences have secured a body of common knowledge and working beliefs as the basis of scholarship and industrial society, not by outward authority or compulsion, but by the convincing power of scientific observation, experiment and discussion. The senses bring a common report of natural phenomena, so as to produce a body of common beliefs. Likewise there are spiritual realities of which the Inner Light gives knowledge. The experiences of the seekers after God bring enough common convictions to form a sufficient basis for group co-operation and fellowship. Like the body of scientific knowledge, these beliefs are subject to continual revision in the larger experiences of religious people; and they are practical because they are grounded on the eternal spiritual verities. "The steps of faith fall on the seeming void, and find the rock beneath."

# IV

## THE THEORY OF WORSHIP

### *Howard H. Brinton, Ph.D.*

Director of Pendle Hill, Graduate School of Religion and
Social Sciences

The Quaker theory and conduct of public worship is the unique contribution which the Society of Friends has made to Christian thought and practice. This method has been approximated in several non-Christian religions and by various societies of mystics within the Christian Church. But Quaker worship contains some features which have never been duplicated. George Fox represents that rare type of religious genius, the experimentalist who makes new discoveries in his field.

In 1643, at the age of nineteen, Fox began his solitary search for Truth. No help came from the professional religious guides whom he consulted. One of his earliest revelations or "openings," as he called them, was "that being bred at Oxford or Cambridge was not enough to fit men to be ministers of Christ." In 1646 occurred the first of Fox's great inner experiences out of which the Quaker way of worship finally emerged. He says in his *Journal*, "I heard a voice which said, 'There is one even Christ Jesus that can speak to thy condition' and when I heard it, my heart did leap for joy.

75

. . . For though I read the scriptures that spake of Christ and of God yet I knew Him not but by revelation."

Not a few of Fox's contemporaries also experienced this mystical revelation of the inner Christ. It was the same phenomenon that sixteen hundred years before had been the central fact of early Christianity. Because of this coincidence, Friends of the first generation of the Society properly called their doctrine "Primitive Christianity Revived." The early Christian Church had lost its Leader in the flesh but He returned as Spirit to inspire His followers. This inspiration was both an individual and a group inspiration. Paul as an individual could write "it pleased God to reveal his Son in me." (Gal. 1:16.) Of the group inspiration he wrote, "The God of our Lord Jesus Christ gave Him to be the head over all things to the church which is His body, the fullness of Him that filleth all in all." (Eph. 1:22, 23.) This belief that the spirit of Christ dwelt in the Church as soul dwells in body, that the Church in fact was the reincarnation of the risen Lord was never wholly lost by Christianity. In Quakerism it received an interpretation somewhat different from that which it received in Catholicism. Protestantism, however, because of its inherent individualism, has provided less explicitly for such a Christ-centered group consciousness.

In Fox's time the Puritans, who were mainly Presbyterians, Independents (Congregationalists), and Particular (Calvinistic) Baptists, had lost awareness of divine Life immanent in the Church. God had, they believed, spoken in times past through the Scriptures and through the finished historic work of Christ. No further revelation was needed or expected until the Second Advent. The troubled times were to many an indication that the Second Coming was near at hand. The business of the Church was to teach men a plan of salvation external to his natural life and experience. Man was totally depraved. He could do nothing to help himself. The revelation to Fox of the inner Christ presented a different picture of divine-human relations. God still spoke to man even as he had spoken of old to the prophets. Salvation became an inner process by which man yielded to divine monitions apprehended within the individual heart.

In interpreting his own religious experience Fox was undoubtedly under the influence of other religious radicals of his time. These thinkers were dissatisfied with the course the Reformation was taking. They were protestants against Protestantism. Their spiritual descent can be traced to heretics who had tried to reform the Church of the Middle Ages. From the early days of the Christian Church there had been a succession of heretical mystical groups, Montanists, Cathari, Waldenses, Beghards and Beguines, Friends of God, Brethren of the Common Life and Anabaptists. All had in common the sense of a Divine-Human Life at the apex of the soul uniting men to God and to each other. The Anabaptists, who formed the mystical left wing of Luther's Reformation, were driven out of Germany. They emigrated to Holland and thence to England. When Cromwell opened the gates of governmental restraint, England swarmed with groups of mystics who asserted to the exasperated Puritans, that the Second Advent had already come in the hearts of men, that God was in His world, speaking to His people. Fox traveled the length and breadth of England in the power of this message.

Yet the message of Quakerism comprised more than just this sense of an inner divine presence. Something more is needed if we are to develop a theory of corporate worship. The doctrine of an individual Inner Light serves well as a basis of individual worship. But if each man follows what appears to him to be his own light and leading, may not confusion result? May not a united worship become impossible? Such confusion did result in the early Church as is evident from Paul's so-called *First Letter to the Corinthians*. To the Puritans, the Quaker doctrine of the Inner Light seemed to be an extreme form of religious individualism resulting in ultimate anarchy. It appeared to make man independent of Church, Book, Society and indeed of every outward control. Religious anarchy was especially characteristic of one English Reformation group called the Ranters. George Fox had many disputes with these enthusiasts. They and other mystical sects of the Commonwealth Period soon withered away but the Quakers survived because they repudiated these anarchistic elements. The original genius of Fox consisted in this: that in an age of increasing individualism he gave to the doctrine of the Inner Light a social rather than an individualized interpretation. This made group worship and an organized society of mystics possible.

The discovery of God within the soul has generally led man to a solitary place where nothing can interfere with perfect enjoyment of this divine experience. "God is most where man is least." The anchorite's cell, the forest hermitage, the lonely mountain or desert place have witnessed raptures in which a mortal has found union with his God. Notable mystics of the East, even more characteristically than those of the West, have insisted on solitariness in the search for this highest of all experiences.

Sometimes for reasons of temporal convenience a group of individuals who are making this lonely search are gathered within a single room. Zen Buddhists in Japan sit together in the Meditation Hall but they do not seek to be welded together as a unit; they are essentially a collection of individuals each making his private search. "It is better when possible," says a Zen scripture, "to sit back to back." In such a "meeting" utterance is unthinkable. Words would but disturb each solitary meditator.

Experience taught early Quakers a type of worship different from that of isolated mystics as well as from that of a collection of equally lonely mystics. Corporate worship in the Society of Friends was not centered in the sacrament, as with Catholics, nor in the sermon, as with the Protestants, but in the "Presence in the midst," that Divine Light illuminating the group and uniting it from above into a single organic whole. Mystical union with God was blended with mystical union with fellow worshipers into a single indivisible experience.

The Friends' meeting for worship is concerned with two relationships as inseparable as are the length and width of an object. The vertical relation to God and the horizontal relation to man are twin co-ordinates in a single frame of reference by which progress in spiritual life can be measured. Each co-ordinate without the other leaves the position undetermined and indefinite. Because the human co-ordinate is necessary in plotting the curve of religious life Quaker mysticism became not only a group mysticism but a group ethical mysticism out of which arose a definite theory of human conduct. Because the divine co-ordinate is also necessary to the frame of reference Quakerism became more than a humanistic ethic. The awe and reverence of the creature in the presence of his Creator, the bowing down of the soul before the Great Mystery, this is the heart of true worship. Through this the soul becomes sensitized to intimations from above which are more than human and without which conduct can have neither goal nor meaning.

## The Theory of Worship

The precise nature of this concept of the divine-human relationship can be understood when we observe the practical way in which Fox and the early Friends analyzed and practiced it. Fox the organizer was quite as significant as Fox the prophet. The first great task was to make converts to the new way. The second great task was to unite these converts into groups which could worship and work together. Fox considered the task of getting them to work together as divinely motivated as the task of getting them to worship together. He writes, "As I had been moved of the Lord to travel in His power round this nation, and in other parts to preach the everlasting gospel and to declare the Word of Life,—so I was afterwards moved to travel, in the same heavenly power, about the nation again (and to write to such places where I came not) to recommend to Friends the setting up of quarterly and monthly meetings in all counties, for looking after the poor, taking care for orderly proceedings in marriage, and other matters relating to the Church of Christ." These so-called "meetings for business" are based on essentially the same principles as the meetings for worship though their object is not primarily the cultivation of inner life but the furnishing of a means through which the inner life of the group can function in practical affairs.

The Quaker meeting for worship may appear at first sight to be founded on a series of negatives. There is no pre-arranged program, no one can tell in advance how the Spirit may guide the worshipers. There is no human head to the meeting, God himself is the Head. There are no outward sacraments, baptism and communion are inward spiritual experiences which find expression in many different outward acts. There are as a rule no hymns, for the spiritual experience expressed by the hymn writer may differ from the spiritual experience of the worshiper. These negative assertions impress the positive fact that spiritual Life is primary and that expressions of it are varied and dependent. A Quaker meeting for worship is an effort to draw from the Spiritual Life at its source and to allow that life natural and spontaneous expression. To determine the type of expression in advance is to reverse this natural order of cause and effect.

Friends wait together in silence but it is a silence of acute awareness and adventurous expectancy. God is in the still small voice heard only in the absence of earthquake, wind and fire. Friends must learn how to be "tender," or "sensitive," to use a more common term, to the faintest monitions of the Spirit heard best in the stillness. Silence is as truly the path to inner life as activity is the path to outer experience. As a camera plate must be surrounded by darkness if it is to become sensitive to light from a single object, so the worshiper must be surrounded by silence when he dares to open that window of the soul through which shines the light of Eternity.

Neither Fox nor his followers left precise directions for practicing the art of worship. We do not find in Quaker literature any description of the various rungs of the Jacob's ladder which reaches up into heaven and down again comparable to that contained in the classic writings of earlier mystics. We have no manuals depicting the stages of ascent such as we find in the voluminous literature of the Yogins of India. Yet, though we find no elaborated system, there are nevertheless in Friends' writings many hints regarding worship.

The worshiper must first, through prayerful striving, be purified and "stripped" of his own narrow, selfish, individual desires and passions. There must be a sinking of one's "own will," a sincere prayer "not my will but Thine be done." To emphasize petty personal interests in the Divine Presence is to attempt to be on a low level and a high level at the same time.

There is nothing original in this process of purification. To attain to any defined objective we must always give up lesser aims. The scholar must give up many enjoyments in order to attain to heights of scholarship. The worshiper must give up selfish desires to attain to the higher life of the Spirit.

Such purification is often followed by new insight in which our partial vision is replaced by a more inclusive view. One sees more widely from a high mountain than when standing in a valley. In this widening of the horizon of knowledge we become more acutely aware of God's presence and of the needs, the sufferings and the joys of our fellows. The worshiper may be silent but his mind is not empty. Past occurrences, present circumstances, possible future events pass before him, but he sees them all now in a new and wider relationship. The problems and sufferings of those around him, the toil of humanity, the life and teaching of Christ, the Divine Power descending from on high, all affect him in a way that would have been impossible in a narrower more specialized state of consciousness. During the days of the week most men must concentrate on a limited area of experience in order to earn the necessities for self-maintenance. In worship each worshiper may widen his experience to include larger and larger areas, perhaps even the whole of life.

This widening of consciousness is not an unusual experience. The writer of a novel may have his attention absorbed by actions of a certain character but he must sometimes turn his mind away from details. He must reconnoiter and survey the plot of his novel as a whole. A scientific worker may be dealing with a mass of apparently unrelated particulars attending first to one and then to another. As he widens his consciousness to include them all he may in a moment of insight find some broad generalization which makes every isolated fact an example of a simple law. So the worshiper may at first find himself baffled by this or that fragment of life which seems to be without meaning. As he rises to a higher and more inclusive perspective he sees life as God sees it and every part acquires new meaning and significance.

The crowning experience in worship is the sense of union with God. Divine Life then floods in and all sense of separateness disappears. Here God is not an object of worship, object and subject are fused into one. God is not brought down to the worshiper, the worshiper is lifted up to God. This is the Quaker communion wherein the communicant takes into himself the substance of deity not as symbolized in bread and wine but as a spiritual presence to pervade his being as fire pervades iron. Before, this experience God was distant, to be supplicated with awe and reverence. Now He appears at the core of one's being, the Soul of the soul, the Self of the self.

Following the Hebrew tradition rather than the Greek the Quaker has usually thought of this union with God as a union of will rather than of substance. God's will may work in and through man when selfish human interests are in abeyance. There is therefore a passive phase as well as an active phase in worship, for God is transcendent as well as immanent. As transcendent, God is above our human thoughts and cannot be reached by human effort alone. The soul may at first struggle toward its goal with such help as sacred writings and inward revelation may afford, but at the end it must quietly wait, its inner temple swept and garnished, ready to receive Him when He wills to come. Such is the testimony of experience as described in Quaker autobiographies. The crowning experience is sometimes interpreted as a state of perfect obedience to the will of God, sometimes as the springing of God's Life and Power within the soul. In either case the worshiper becomes God-centered rather than self-centered.

Many deny that this highest experience of union with God is possible except to a few exceptional persons. Yet it is probably a common possibility though not always recognized for what it is. Here, as in the case of "purification" and "enlightenment" we are not dealing with exceptional instances. A group of persons may be striving for some objective. At first the members may appear alien and separate. They co-operate because of belief in what they are doing. But a time may come when they forget themselves completely, when each isolated self is transcended and all are fused into one. Thus an athlete playing on a team may at first feel his separate individuality but as the game progresses he may become as fully a part of the whole team as an arm is part of a human body. By similar token and in a more significant way the worshiper finds his isolated self transcended through an experience which makes him one with God.

Purification, enlightenment, union,—these are the three states in the Pilgrim's Progress of the soul, often described in the writings of the great mystics. These three also have their place in the worship of the Society of Friends. They are described under many names in the voluminous literature of its three hundred years of religious experience. But a description of worship in these terms alone emphasizes its individual rather than its corporate aspect. The Quaker practice of group silence cannot forbid each individual to go his own way but it places greater emphasis on a process in which the worshipers may seek adjustments with each other through God or they may seek God through adjustments with each other. The search for the ultimate goal of union with God includes a search for organic unity of the group.

The biological term "organic" is here used as a figure of speech which can be extended to apply to many levels of existence. Some writers consider an atom or a molecule to be "organic" as the whole is more than the sum of its parts. In the case of people we find that a group may be bound together internally in such a way that the whole is more than the sum of its parts and that each part becomes both means and end.[1] The method by which this is accomplished includes more than the establishment of horizontal relations between individuals. There must also be a vertical relation of all the persons to something qualitatively different and higher than any. The athletic team is welded together by an objective which means more than does any individual on the team. This objective is the attainment of victory. A group working for a

[1] For a further exposition of this theory of worship see H. H. Brinton, *Creative Worship*, Allen and Unwin, 1931.

cause is united, not by the members watching each other but by the absorption of each in the super-individual cause. A meeting for worship is united not by an abstract impersonal cause but by the worship of God who transcends all causes. Through this worship the individual is self-transcended. He becomes a cell in a super-personal organism, which is more than the sum of its parts. This *More* which is added is divine and comes down from above. A meeting, it is true, often fails to achieve unity of this type because some individuals cannot rise out of the individualistic plane, but the possibility of failure in no way invalidates our striving toward the goal.

If the meeting for worship is an organism we should expect it to have a certain size in which it functions best. Experience shows that this size is small—perhaps a group of from twenty to fifty persons.

In those types of religious worship which assign the leadership to a priest or minister, unity is attained by following that leadership. Such a unity is comparatively easy to secure and does not therefore seem to be a desired end to be striven for as prerequisite to worship. The need for interhuman adjustments does not strikingly appear because nearly all the adjustments are made to the leader and his teachings. If there is no externally imposed unity, as is the case in a Quaker meeting, the congregation must wait for the slow, silent, uncertain growth of organic relations from within. This internal unity is more difficult to achieve but it recognizes frankly that religion is a matter of inter-human relations as well as of divine-human relations. "First be reconciled to thy brother and then come and offer thy gift."

Protestantism attained strength through emphasis upon the vertical relation, that of the individual worshiper to his transcendent God. God's glory, His Holiness, utter submission of the worshiper to His Will which is above human understanding; these have been the ennobling concepts which have given power to Protestant worship. Each man stands alone in the sight of heaven. Alone, from the City of Destruction to the Heavenly Jerusalem, Bunyan's pilgrim makes his progress. A modern reaction against this severe individualism is the Social Gospel as it is often preached from pulpits today. Urgently as we need a social gospel, the message and the reality of "good tidings to the poor," the atmosphere of reaction should not turn mankind from that awe and wonder and sense of mystery which were so strikingly characteristic of early Protestantism. A social gospel tends to degenerate into a system of ethics. This result sometimes besets organized Protestant churches because there has been no blending of the vertical and horizontal relations in a single experience. Quaker theory and practice aims not only to think but to feel unity both with mankind and with God. There must be a mystical apprehension of the unity of all life in

God if religion is to be lifted above the plane of ethics without ceasing to be ethical.

Catholic worship, expressed in sacrament, religious instruction and liturgy, takes an intermediate place between Protestant and Quaker worship in its ability to rise above the mechanical level on which the congregation is a collection of individuals to the organic realm in which the members are united with God and each other. Sacrament and liturgy in which a whole congregation mystically shares are a powerful uniting force. Through it the worshiper is brought into the awful presence of the great mystery which the solemn words and acts both conceal and express. It is not necessary that words or acts possess an intellectual meaning. The Catholic priest chanting in Latin or the Buddhist priest chanting in Sanskrit speaks not to the mind but to the heart. In that heart-worship individual loneliness is overcome.

Yet there are in the present scientific age serious difficulties and dangers in a sacramental and liturgical type of worship. Many people today find its forms outworn and meaningless. It tends to exert an esthetic rather than a distinctly religious appeal. It may not arise spontaneously from the heart because it is often the expression of the characteristic spirit of a bygone age. For this reason it is in danger of becoming an outwardly imposed process to be gone through by rote. However, in spite of these difficulties a noble liturgy is now and will always be the Bread of Life to many, for the language of the heart is the same in all ages. In Catholic worship the sermon plays a minor part, in Protestant worship historically it holds the leading role. But today many Protestant churches are endeavoring to get away from a sermon-centered type of public worship. More liturgy is being introduced and, in several instances, altar has replaced pulpit in the central position.

Some writers have characterized the Quaker way as a liturgical silence. Silence, it is true, is a form, but it is a form which does not lack possibilities of sacredness or meaning to the modern mind. An instance of this is the fact that commemoration of the armistice of 1918 takes the form of a brief silence throughout this and other lands. Silence is based on no dogmatic assertions. Its principal weakness is that it is so liable to failure in producing the desired response. With an outwardly imposed pattern one can predict what will happen but with dependence on "inner guidance" the worshiper is launched on uncharted ways. A Quaker meeting is an adventure which may end no one knows where, perhaps nowhere.

Yet this uncertainty as to outcome is also a basis of strength. More is risked, more can be gained. Because a silent meeting is not programmed in advance it is more likely to be creative of the new and unpredictable than other forms of worship. Creativity results from spontaneity and freedom.

The power to create also depends on a living synthesis of diverse elements. A meeting controlled by an individual or by a program seldom produces what is not already in that individual or program. If, however, many individuals, each sensitive to the Light of Truth, bring together their diversity of tendencies and possibilities, something new may emerge more inclusive and hence more "true" than any one point of view. This is brought about, not by a mechanical juxtaposition of different opinions but by a real fusion. One may mix oxygen and hydrogen and obtain nothing new. But apply a flame and the new substance, water, is created.

So indeed the flame of the Spirit that creates the Universe will unite many partial human views into one divine whole of Truth. The change is not quantitative but qualitative. The Spirit does not add, it transforms. The congregation may be lifted up to a higher level of life which is in the world, but not of it. As mind emerges if animal cells are united in certain configurations called brains, spirit emerges if human beings are united in certain configurations of worship. This process, seen from within, is found to be, not creation by the worshipers alone, but the descent of Spirit from above as the tongues of fire descended on the day of Pentecost.

It may be that the divine fire will first touch some individual who may feel constrained to speak to the meeting. A communication will follow in which this human instrument endeavors to interpret the message which has arisen from within. The Quaker sermon is a peculiar utterance. It does not ordinarily fulfill the function of a sermon in a Protestant church. Its object is not essentially to teach. George Fox said that it was the task of the minister to "take men to Christ and leave them there"; to direct men to the Divine Teacher, not to teach them himself. "Mind the admonitions of the Lord within you," is a frequent word of counsel. He who preaches does not argue, arguments generally suggest counter opinions. When William Penn asked George Fox whether or not he should continue to wear his sword Fox replied, "Wear it as long as thou can'st." Fox did not argue regarding the futility of war. He directed Penn to his inner guide. This type of ministry aims primarily to increase the sensitivity of the worshiper.

But there are other types of spiritual utterance. Social and personal problems may be brought before the meeting if they are not brought in a spirit of controversy or debate but in awe and humility and a deep religious sense of the mystery of Divine Truth. In the presence of the God of the Universe a problem previously seen from a narrow selfish viewpoint acquires new meaning. True worship produces a widening of consciousness, a view more inclusive than those specialized standpoints which can be designated as economic, political or scientific. It is no light thing to break the silence. The speaker should be brief and to the point. If his communication appears to his fellow worshipers as "out of the Life," that is, as striking a jarring or discordant note, it is their religious duty lovingly to inform him of the fact at some suitable time after the meeting is over. This process of "eldering" however should not be merely repressive. Sometimes those who do not speak when they ought to speak need encouragement to be faithful to the call to service.

This dependence of the worshipers upon each other is based on the belief that the Divine Light which shines within is not exclusively an individual light. It illumines the whole group. The revelation which any individual has received should accordingly be checked by the revelations to others. The detection of personal responsibility is a task of extreme delicacy. In the face of it a human being may well quake. As in a family one counsels another, so brethren in Christ must encourage and uphold. When an individual has a "concern" to enter upon some special service, it is usually the Quaker practice to lay that concern before the meeting and to go forward with it only if the meeting concurs. In rare cases, however, an unusual degree of certainty may lead to something in word or deed that is beyond the stage of development of the meeting as a whole.

In view of such practices the social significance of Quaker worship becomes apparent.[2] A primary object of worship is to realize in experience the ties which bind human beings together. It is one thing to believe in God because some say He exists.

[2] See H. H. Brinton, *A Religious Solution to the Social Problem*, Pendle Hill, 1934.

94

It is another thing to know Him directly. It is one thing to be told that all men are brothers, it is another thing to sense it as a present fact. In worship the unity of all life in God is apprehended directly. It is not something to be argued about and proved.

Men may work together because they are compelled to do so by a governing power. Or they may co-operate because of enlightened self-interest, persuaded that there is more to be gained by co-operation than by conflict. But a higher stage is reached when men sense their inherent relation to each other, the brotherliness which makes them all children of a common Father. Conflict between men then becomes as useless and absurd as conflict between different parts of a single bodily frame.

Quaker worship is the basis of Quaker pacifism. I cannot fight with another man any more than I can fight with myself, once I have discovered that the same divine Light shines in all, or, to use a hallowed figure, once I have perceived that all are branches of the One Vine. In worship we become aware that the same life-giving sap flows through all the branches. This is revealed not from without as a fact to be mentally accepted by reason, but from within as a principle of which our knowledge is first-hand. When it fulfills its ideals the Quaker meeting becomes a kind of germ cell of a true human society wherein men are united not outwardly by constraint but inwardly by the sharing of a common Life. It becomes a kind of training ground for citizens of the Kingdom of God. The adjustments which human beings make to each other in a spirit of worship do not involve domination of one or another individual or one idea as against others or even the domination of a majority over a minority. Every individual becomes both end and means in a larger whole of life. This is the ideal type of society in which individualism is overcome not by dominance which suppresses but by love which fulfills.

The Quaker may go forth from his meeting resolved to create with his fellowmen outside the same type of relationship which has been created with his fellow worshipers in the meeting. This is a difficult task but the fact that such relations have already been created with some men makes it appear more feasible for them to be created with others. The same methods may not be applicable outside the meeting as inside it, but similar methods are possible. One can always appeal to the light of God shining in the other man. Such faith both creates and reveals what it looks for. Here again immediate failure is more probable than when violent or mechanical methods are used, but when success is attained the results are immeasurably more significant and more lasting.

Primitive man was less individualistic than modern man. He was better able to sense the inner unity of humanity. His religious rites took the form of means to create and increase the sense of unity. When man became more individualistic he looked back on these early days of communal consciousness as a "golden age," a "Garden of Eden" which has been lost. The "Fall of Man" was the coming of an individual self-consciousness through which came loneliness and a sense of separation from God and our fellows. Today as always, religion seeks to transcend this individualism by uniting the individual with a larger whole of Life.

But with primitive man this larger whole of Life was felt in a biological sense. The tribe was a large family, its religion brought unity only within the particular tribe. It did not bring unity with other tribes. Rather it accentuated enmity toward those with whom no ties of kinship existed. For example, early worship of Jehovah united Israel. Jehovah was the Lord of Hosts, the leader in Israel's wars against her enemies. A more mature religion has a larger and more difficult task. Its God is not a tribal or national deity, but God of the universe. The human unity sought for is not biological, it is spiritual. Through Christ Judaism evolved into a world religion and the prayer of Christ that "they all may be one" was not meant in any tribal or in any national sense. Because the Society of Friends is a Society of Christians they seek in worship for that unity which is not denominational, or tribal, or racial, or national, but universal, for the Light of Christ enlightens "every man that cometh into the world." Therefore Friends are pacifists and internationalists.

The meeting for worship is the chief instrument toward this end. It inculcates sensitive awareness to forces and influences not easily felt in the ordinary workaday world. Sensitivity is the most important of all human qualities. In the long process of evolution human beings and their subhuman ancestors have out-classed their rivals because they were more sensitive. Not only does this apply to bodily sensitivity but even more explicitly to keen awareness to the needs of others and most of all to a sense of Life as a whole. This is the general thesis of Gerald Heard in his book entitled *The Source of Civilization*. It is the meek, he shows, not the callous or those who are sensitive only to their personal wants, who inherit the earth. The specialist is handicapped because he is sensitive to a limited aspect of reality. The sensitive human hand is not specialized as is the comparatively insensitive claw or fin or wing. Because our ancestors possessed members sensitive to a wide realm of reality they suffered more than did other creatures, but they survived while beings which became insensitive to anything outside their own specialty could not adapt themselves to changes of condition and went under when changes occurred.

Sensitivity is the prerequisite of progress and the chief product of a type of life which finds its culmination in worship. That the type of worship we are discussing is successful in producing sensitivity is shown by the fact that the Quakers have been pioneers in several reforms such as religious liberty, humane treatment of the insane and of criminals, the abolition of slavery, and the promotion of peace. Testimonies which are commonplaces today were not so when first advocated by Friends. The history of the Society is a clear indication that mysticism under certain conditions may have important social consequences.

There is a certain type of insensitivity today which accounts for one of the chief problems of modern man. As man progresses in science and in the art of using tools to control both nature and his fellow man his attention becomes almost exclusively centered on the world around him. He is a specialist in one aspect of reality—the objective world as revealed by his senses. But the outer world is only a part and perhaps the least important part of reality. It is a world of means, not of ends; of tools, not of objectives; of facts, not of values.

There are at least two serious results of this exclusive attention focused upon the outer world. Being insensitive to the inner world in which man feels his unity with a larger whole of Life he knows only the outer world in which men are tools to be used or obstacles in the path to be removed by force. Society based on violence lacks inner cohesion and tends to fall apart. The only external remedy by which anarchy can be averted is the continuous application of force. The age of increasing individualism which began with Renaissance and Reformation has reached its climax and a new collectivism is arising based, not on inner spiritual ties, but on an increase of external authority. Dictatorships are replacing democracies. It is a widely held belief that a disintegrating society can be saved by laws and programs or by powerful leaders. Yet nothing can be more certain than that a society which has no inner cohesion cannot last. The time has gone by when inner cohesion can be produced by biological factors. Inner cohesion today is one of the products of inwardly directed spiritual life in which the unity of mankind in God is realized.

The other serious consequence of exclusive attention to the outer world is that man is thrown out of balance. Only one side of himself is developed. As an athlete may devolop one part of his frame out of proportion to the rest of his body, so man today develops only the outer crust of his mind and neglects the whole interior of his being. As a result, a large proportion of modern men are suffering from a neurosis. Life has lost its meaning. Knowledge of the meaning of life comes from inner experience. Without such experience life will either collapse like a shell without inner substance or develop a type of activity which is essentially pathological because it is aimless. To regain our balance, to feel life in its wholeness, to restore value and meaning to existence, we must develop a technique for the enhancement of the inner life.

Such a technique has long been known in the

East. The Yogins of India, the Chan Buddhists of China and their brothers the Zen Buddhists of Japan are experts in the exploration and cultivation of the inner life. But these religionists have neglected the outer man quite as much as the West has neglected the inner. As a consequence their religious experience is lacking in ethical consequences. They are willing to devote their lives to teaching to others the truth they have learned, but they have few plans for a better human society.

There is evident today an increasing reaction in the West against exclusive attention to the outward. It shows itself in various unhealthy ways such as occultism. There are said to be more astrologers, necromancers, and fortune tellers carrying on their divinations today than at any time since the sixteenth century. A higher evidence of attention to the inner is the progress of psychoanalysis. Psychoanalysis is an endeavor to explore the unseen depths of the inner life, to eliminate from it evils which produce disturbances, and to encourage the growth of that which will harmonize and integrate. Psychologists have shown that the inner depths contain both demons and angels. Man can have either at his service.

Because the inner life contains both good and evil and is both super-human and sub-human, psychologists will never completely solve the problem which troubles modern man. Psychology in its scientific aspect deals with facts rather than with values. It can reveal the lowly origin of some thoughts and feelings but it cannot generate the power by which man can rise to higher thoughts and feelings. To know the highest is not necessarily to love it. Something more than knowledge is required. Great religions of the world all exist for the purpose of enabling man to live according to the highest that is in him. The highest must not only be revealed but must exert the power to attract and uplift. This Highest is not revealed in the visible world outside. Christians believe that the Highest was once incarnate in a visible life. That historical revelation still has power to draw men upward. That the cosmic Christ is revealed within is also an essential of Christianity. In worship we find at the apex of the soul Divine Power lifting us upward. In so doing it unites us with all who share this higher Life.

If we are to discover that Vine which alone unites the branches, if we are to become aware of a vital, inner, cohesive power to heal a disintegrating society, if we are to restore to modern man in the western world the balance lost because of a too exclusive attention to the outward, we must find a way to reveal and develop those areas of the soul which have been neglected. There is every reason to believe that these areas will bear the same rich fruits as in the past. Man has wandered far from that spiritual home which nurtured him in his youth and which sent him forth, a lonely individual, to try his fortunes in the world around him. He cannot return to the home he left, but he can build a new one where the same fire shall burn upon the hearth and where the same potent sense of family solidarity shall have widened to include mankind.

# THE QUAKER METHOD OF REACHING DECISIONS

## D. Elton Trueblood, Ph.D.

### Professor of the Philosophy of Religion, Stanford University

"Friends are not to meet like a company of people about town or parish business, neither in their men's nor women's meetings, but to wait upon the Lord."—*George Fox,* 1675.

THE present generation has become uniquely conscious of the technique of group discussion, a technique which has often been used successfully in the past though it has seldom been the subject of deliberate study. In this century there is growing up an ambitious literature concerned with the conference method,[1] and several persons have developed great skill in the guidance of group thinking. The basic conviction which is the occasion for this growing body of literature is the idea that the search for truth on the part of a group may be quite different from, and often more successful than, the same search when carried on by individuals in isolation. The various members of the group present their thoughts as they arise and these stimulate thoughts in others. The result is that many suggestions appear which were not in the minds of any when the search began. Sometimes it is quite

[1] A descriptive bibliography may be found in *The Art of Conference,* by Frank Walser.

104

impossible to give individual credit for opinions which all eventually share though originally held by none. The skillful leader of such a discussion group does not present his own preconceived notions, but tries to stimulate thought by piercing questions or the balancing of opinions as they appear. He is not the master of the group, but more truly its servant, providing the necessary link for co-operative thinking. Like the Platonic Socrates the group discussion leader's purpose is not to present formed and finished ideas of his own, but to be a spiritual midwife, helping the members of the group to bear their own intellectual children.

We must guard against the over-enthusiastic notion that this conference method is applicable to all problems. It is not applicable, for example, to problems which demand technical information. It is surely a delusion to suppose that the pooling of ignorance will produce information. But, with this warning in mind, we may safely proceed to see what genuine sharing of thought can accomplish under able guidance. In any case it is easier, in most fields, to secure information than to achieve clarity of thought. Many can give testimony to the fact that this method of group search, while it can fail miserably, can also reach splendid heights and become genuinely *creative*. Indeed an harmonious, thinking group is one of the best illustrations of creative synthesis. An individual in a thoughtful group is not the same as an individual

105

alone, because there is an emergent quality which the fact of "togetherness" releases. Often the ideas which come to the individual in the group are original in the sense that they have not been directly suggested by others, but they come to the individual as a result of what another says. The very attempt to state a thought clearly may add to the clarity with which it is held, and so the creative process continues.

In much of the literature dealing with the method of discussion leadership and the stimulating experience of membership in a seeking group, reference is made to the experience of the Society of Friends.[2] The references, however, are usually brief and thus cannot be expected to give any adequate sense of what is peculiar in the Quaker contribution to the subject. The purpose of this essay is to give to those, already interested in the general conception of co-operative thinking, an introduction to essentials of the Quaker conference procedure, prefaced by some idea of how the method arose, and followed by some examples of how it has worked in practice.

I

When the Quaker Movement began in the middle of the seventeenth century in England it was

[2] Characteristic references are H. S. Elliott, *The Process of Group Thinking,* New York, 1928, p. 72, and Frank Walser, *The Art of Conference,* New York, 1933, pp. 24, 26, 285.

what may be termed "spiritual" empiricism. There were two convictions which towered above all others in the estimation of George Fox and his intimate associates. These were:

(1) Religion is centered in first-hand *experience,* rather than in "notions" (intellectual formulations) or in external forms and practices.

(2) Revelation is continuous and immediate, never confined to a single country, period or nation.

The combination of these two convictions breeds many other convictions, especially concerning the value of the individual, irrespective of his learning or ordination or lack of these. The devout Christian can and should expect as close a relationship with God as was known by those who wrote the Bible. Christ is as truly able to lead His followers today as when He walked in Palestine. The "Real Presence" is a perennial possibility, not especially in bread and wine, but in any features of our ordinary workaday world.

It is easy to see that this was a thrilling gospel in the seventeenth century, as indeed it is in any century.

When we read the voluminous literature of the first generation of Friends our attention is quickly drawn to the note of authority with which they spoke and wrote. The priests and ministers quoted the works of divines or the Bible, but Friends had no doubt that they spoke as they were divinely instructed. A man in this mood could stand firm in spite of the magistrates who sent him to prison and in spite of the theologians who presented long arguments. It might seem that the logical result of such a movement would be sheer anarchy, in which no person would pay attention to the insights of his fellows.

If Quakerism had adopted the individualistic interpretation there would now be no Quakerism to discuss. Since it is inherent in the position that there can be no curb on fanaticism, the convictions of the various Friends would have canceled each other. In fact there were many other religious movements which arose at the same time and which disappeared as soon as the first flush of enthusiasm was over. An important question for the historian concerns the reason for Quakerism's success in contrast with the failure of apparently similar movements. The question was well stated by the mathematician, Augustus De Morgan:

"Fox and Muggleton are men of one type, developed by the same circumstances: it is for those who investigate such men to point out why their teachings have had fates so different. Macaulay says it was because Fox found followers of more sense than himself. True enough, but why did Fox find such followers and not Muggleton? The two were equally crazy, to all appearance: and the difference required must be sought in the doctrines themselves." [3]

[3] Augustus De Morgan, *A Budget of Paradoxes,* London, 1872, pp. 245, 246.

The Muggletonians declined rapidly after the death of the founder of the sect, Ludowick Muggleton, but were not extinct in the nineteenth century.

# The Quaker Method of Reaching Decisions

If we search for the added element in the teaching of early Friends which saved their movement from the natural fate of uncritical fanaticism, we find it in the idea of the "group." If the revelation of God's will is continuous and immediate, it demands some instrument, and that instrument may be a group of seekers as truly as it may be a lone individual.

One of the first Friends to see and state clearly the possibility of group revelation was Isaac Penington. Penington was eight years older than Fox and a man of great cultural opportunities, but he did not hesitate long to accept the leadership of Fox when he once heard Fox's message. He agreed that all creeds, all sacraments, and even the Scriptures are secondary; he recognized that it is possible to go beyond all interpretations to Christ Himself. But though he agreed in this central emphasis Penington had a keener sense of the difficulty of knowing what is true or right. He knew that there is a discipline for knowledge, whether it be knowledge of scientific matters or spiritual matters. Thus the individual might be mistaken in spite of his mood of confidence. Penington's words are still a sober warning:

"It is not an easie matter, in all cases clearly and understandingly to discern the Voice of the Shepherd, the Motions of God's Spirit, and certainly to distinguish the Measure of Life from all other Voices, Motions and Appearances whatsoever. Through much growth in the Truth, through much waiting on the Lord, through much Fear and Trembling, through much Sobriety and Meekness, through much exercise of the

Senses this is at length given and obtained. And yet there is a preservation in the meantime." [4]

Part of this "preservation in the meantime" is the wisdom which comes by means of corporate guidance. Penington held, as firmly as did Fox, to the reality of divine leadership, but he had a deep sense of the fact that the understanding of God's will, though possible, *is not easy*. Since our "openings" may not be genuine, we should therefore let our openings be judged by the Lord. But how are we to know? The will of the Lord is to be known "even by his pure Life and Spirit in his People."

In these fertile words lies the seed of the whole conception of group judgment which the Society of Friends has developed. Friends at the beginning were faced with a dilemma: either they must accept the validity of external authority (whether Romanist or Protestant) or they had no check on the spirit of libertines and Ranters. The deep Quaker conviction was that these two horns of the dilemma did not exhaust the possibilities. They felt there should be a better way and their very expectancy helped them to formulate it. The fundamental solution included the setting aside of times for group judgment upon matters affecting both individuals and the group, the decision to be rendered not by a vote at the conclusion of a par-

[4] Isaac Penington. *Some Queries concerning the Order and Government of the Church of Christ*. This publication was not dated, but was "written in Alisbury Prison," probably in 1666.

liamentary debate, but by a joint decision of the entire group as the result of approaching each problem in the mood of reverent search for God's will.

It is clear that the Quaker method of group decision arose spontaneously just as did the Quaker manner of worship which is described elsewhere in this volume. In Barclay and Penn we find arguments for the method, but they were only giving rational justification to what was already an accepted practice when they wrote. The immense belief of Friends in the reality of continued revelation made them expect a revelation of God's will in a group meeting. They accordingly arranged the group meeting in a manner best calculated to know the revelation if it was forthcoming.

The theory of group decision on this basis found an able and persuasive exponent in the person of Robert Barclay. Barclay is famous for his *Apology,* but an earlier book, *The Anarchy of the Ranters* (1674), is of great value and gives the theory of Quaker group organization. Barclay was especially aware of the dangers of libertinism, apparently much exercised by the outcroppings of this spirit in the infant Quaker Movement. Some had gone so far as to appear naked in public places, holding that they were led of God to make such a demonstration for a spiritual purpose.[5]

Barclay was quick to note a similar need of

[5] Cf. W. C. Braithwaite, *The Second Period of Quakerism,* London, 1919, p. 25.

spiritual government in the early Christian Church, as described in the New Testament, and was convinced that the Quaker practice was none other than a return to the primitive Christian model. The early Christians did not have an intricate system of offices and delegation of powers, but met together quite simply, as a group of humble followers of Christ, to try to learn the leading of the Spirit. Barclay believed the time had again come when Christians could meet in little, intimate groups, quite as simply and quite as expectantly, and that the Divine Message would be given. The whole conception is put tersely in the following paragraph:

"If so be, in such a church there should arise any difference, there will be an infallible judgment from the Spirit of God, which may be in a general assembly; yet not limited to it, as excluding others: and may prove the judgment of the plurality; yet not to be decided thereby, as if the infallibility were placed there, excluding the fewer. In which meeting or assembly upon such an account, there is no limitation to be of persons particularly chosen; but that all that in a true sense may be reckoned of the Church, as being sober and weighty, may be present and give their judgment." [6]

II

The method of group decision has not been changed in its essentials since Barclay wrote, but his brief statement does not give an adequate conception of what the method is. This method is a unique form of the general conference method,

[6] Robert Barclay, *The Anarchy of the Ranters,* Section VIII.

marked by four conditions, all of which are necessary. These four conditions refer to (1) the nature
of the group, (2) the mood of the gathering, (3)
the qualifications for participation, and (4) the
method of ascertaining the decision. These will be
discussed in the order named.

(1) *Group solidarity* is assumed in the use of
the Quaker method. The group is not of any specified number, though normally it is small enough
so that it does not seem like a "mass meeting." Perhaps the average number is forty or fifty. It is expected that these persons who make up the group
shall already have many experiences and convictions in common. They are bound together by affection for each other and by adherence to a common faith. Frequently, many of them are neighbors in a single community. Ideally the fellowship
is intimate, so that the various members really care
about each other. There are many Quaker groups
in which this condition is lacking, and when it is
conspicuously lacking, the entire method breaks
down.

(2) *The expectation of corporate guidance* is
central to the mood of the Quaker gathering.
Friends have a strong conviction, when differences
arise, that there is a right way and that this may
well be shown to them if they are sufficiently sensitive. This is why decision is often postponed
when there is a marked division in the group. If
there is a live possibility of finding a way which
will convince the entire group of its rightness, we

are foolish to be satisfied with makeshifts or compromises. The very unwillingness to accept low standards is an important factor in any conference and the spirit of expectancy is itself creative of what is expected.

In view of these considerations we can see how similar the mood of the Quaker discussion is to that of worship and how alien to the debating mood. The debater seeks to win, but the worshiper seeks to listen and to share. "These meetings are opened, and usually concluded," wrote William Penn, "in their solemn waiting upon God, who is sometimes graciously pleased to answer them with as signal evidences of his love and presence as in any of their meetings for worship." [7]

Though the problems faced are often those having to do with the practical aspects of life, they are approached in the spirit of prayer and devotion. Secular matters are to be decided in a spiritual atmosphere, or, what is much the same, we are to renounce the secular conception entirely.

It is perfectly consistent with the Quaker conference method for someone to vocalize prayer in the midst of ordinary deliberations. Often, when a problem is particularly difficult, especially when there are strong sympathies on opposite sides, someone will rise and suggest that the entire assembly give up speaking or arguing and join in

[7] William Penn, *The Rise and Progress of the People called Quakers,* Philadelphia, 1849, p. 47.

a time of quiet waiting on God. It has often been true that this has brought unity. Sometimes a new idea comes out of the quiet waiting that is different from both ideas for which there has been contention, an idea to which both parties can agree.

Ideally the group decisions should deal with all kinds of problems in practical life. Among Friends they have long dealt with marriage, as is shown in another chapter of the present volume. The person wishing to marry presents his intention to his group and seeks the approbation of the group. If the approbation is forthcoming the group finally witnesses to the vows of the couple and the marriage is an accomplished fact. Could not the question of a life work be brought before the group with equal appropriateness? Surely it would be wise to get all possible help in such important matters, raising all major decisions to the plane of the sacred.

(3) *All present may share in the deliberations of the group,* regardless of age, sex or education. In many gatherings for discussion participation is based upon the holding of office or being elected as a delegate, but Friends, from the beginning, have adopted a platform of radical democracy. It is true that representatives to Quarterly and Yearly Meetings of Friends are appointed, but the representatives have no superior status and the appointment is made merely to ensure adequate attendance. It is not expected that there will be any onlookers at a meeting of this kind, but that all will be participators, either actual or potential.

This general participation, on the part of ordinary persons, raises the average interest and thus makes a situation in which exceptional genius is more likely to appear. A body made up of the rank and file is strikingly different from one made up of delegates or of those whose religion is in any sense professional. In the words of Barclay, none is to be excluded, "whether married, or a tradesman, or a servant." Thus there may be a note of reality which is quite lacking in assemblies made up of those who have had ordination or belong to a special succession. Sometimes the unlearned have valuable insights which great learning tends to hinder.

(4) *The "sense of the meeting" is the basis of decision,* rather than a division into majority and minority. This sense of the meeting is practical unanimity and failure to arrive at it is usually the occasion for postponement. Each group has a "clerk," a person appointed to fill the double office of chairman and secretary. The clerk is appointed, not to guide the discussion, but to make a faithful record of what the real convictions of the group are. His main qualification is sensitiveness to what others think.

When the group is already in the mood akin to worship, which is described above, a subject is presented for consideration, often by means of some written communication which has come to the clerk's desk. No one is prodded to speak and all wait quietly until someone rises and makes a suggestion regarding the problem in hand. This will be the occasion for a contribution from some other person. It might be supposed that, with such freedom, there would be several trying to speak at once. Actually, however, the general note of high seriousness is a more effective check on such tendencies than any external rule could be, and the note of reality is strengthened by the absence of the barren formality of parliamentary rules of order.

Often, as various persons speak freely, it becomes evident that there is a marked division in the group. If this continues, the clerk makes no minute, but often suggests that the group might well turn to another matter. Normally, however, the very freedom and sobriety of the discussion lead the participators to some new position which is genuinely uniting. Then the clerk, when he thinks this time has come, makes a minute, stating what he conceives the group conviction to be. The clerk sometimes makes errors of judgment, but remarkably seldom is any criticism of this kind made. The whole setting helps the clerk to rise above his ordinary capacity. This interpretation of the sense of the meeting, made without hurry at the clerk's desk, often receives some verbal modification from voluntary suggestions made when it is read, and sometimes the substance is modified, but ordinarily the judgment of the clerk is acepted as a valid statement of the situation. It is understood that the clerk has considered the spiritual experience of those who have spoken, but has not counted heads nor judged by official positions held. Above all, it is understood that he is recording the judgment of the group *as a group* and not the judgment of isolated individuals. It is known that decisions are reached jointly which never could have been reached separately. A clerk cannot get the sense of the meeting by calling the members on the telephone and asking their opinions, as is sometimes done in committee work. Friends expect a creative development of thought as men and women search together.

The experience of an early stage of strong differences of opinion followed by a later stage of the discussion in which the differences are overcome by a deeper understanding occurs so often that Friends expect it. The point is that they *wait* for this culmination. If a vote were taken in the early stages there might be a fairly large minority which would henceforth look upon itself as the defeated party, with attendant hard feeling. The Quaker method is calculated to discourage the development of party spirit within the group. Then the discussion is not devoted to the winning of a party victory, but to the ascertainment of the truth.

This method of decision thus described is closely allied to pacifism as a method of life. Pacifism is more than mere refusal to participate in war, and is a method by which men can live in all circumstances including the circumstance of group decision. Pacifism means the use of love and persuasion as against force and violence. The overpowering of a minority by calling for a vote is a kind of force, and breeds the resentment which keeps the method of force from achieving ultimate success with persons. "You have not converted a man," wrote John Morley, "because you have silenced him." [8]

### III

It is not difficult to find splendid illustrations of the way in which the Quaker method of group decision works, particularly because of the ample records that Friends have kept for the greater part of three centuries. It must be admitted that the method has sometimes broken down completely, and today we should not, like Barclay, use the word infallible in connection with the method. The extreme cases in which the method has failed have been those resulting in separation. The condition most lacking in such cases was the one we have mentioned as the second condition. When separations occurred the mood of the gatherings has ceased to have any kinship to the mood of worship.

Some of the best illustrations of the method have been in regard to problems of theological belief. In 1887 there was a large gathering of representatives of Friends from many parts of America and the British Isles at Richmond, Indiana, the purpose of the gathering being the promulga-

[8] John Morley, *On Compromise,* London, 1917, p. 246.

tion of some statement of belief calculated to draw groups more closely together. The plan had its dangers, however, especially in view of the fact that the Quaker Movement has never submitted to a written creed. Those who favored the statement feared looseness of belief and those who opposed it feared the substitution of dogmatic correctness for immediate experience of God. An English writer, Edward Grubb, has told how the proposition was handled, according to the Quaker method, in his own country.

"As a young man I was deeply impressed by a debate in London Yearly Meeting on the Richmond Declaration of Faith (1888), when the effort was made by a number of leading Friends to promote (as they thought) the unity of "orthodox" Friends throughout the world by the adoption of an elaborate statement of belief. The proposal aroused intense feeling on both sides. It was debated for a whole day in a crowded meeting of over one thousand Friends (men and women), every one of whom had the right to speak; and in the end the whole meeting fully accepted the decision of the clerk that it was not prepared to adopt the Declaration." [9]

At Baltimore Yearly Meeting the same problem came up in the late autumn of 1887. In Baltimore, as in London, there were strong convictions on both sides, but finally the meeting reached a generally accepted conclusion that the Declaration be approved *but not adopted*. That is, they expressed their belief in the ideas which the Declaration included without making it into an official test of membership. This eminently sane solution of the problem was reached by means of vigorous

[9] Edward Grubb, *What is Quakerism*, London, 1919, pp. 96, 97.

discussion and the meeting concluded in the spirit of worship.[10]

Some striking examples of the use of the method may be gathered from the All Friends Peace Conference which was held in London in 1920. At that time there was such serious friction with Russia that many thought war between England and Russia was a live possibility. The "Council of Action," representing Labor, sought to keep Britain out of war by refusing to make or handle munitions for use abroad. It was early proposed that the Conference should send a letter to the Council of Action sanctioning the stand they were taking. Many were afraid this would be tantamount to active sympathy with the Russian side of the dispute. After much vigorous discussion with a strongly marked division of judgment and much patience, the clerk finally drafted a minute from which there was no dissent. The following testimony of a member of the Conference is impressive:

"It is clear that if the method of the vote had been used when the proposal was first brought forward, and indeed at any time until the final session was reached, whichever view had been carried, the vote would have split the Conference. The method of further waiting to seek for light resulted in an agreed decision because the Conference as a whole had by now reached the conviction that the proposal was right." [11]

[10] Anna B. Thomas, *Life and Letters of Richard H. Thomas, M.D.*, Philadelphia, 1905, p. 219.

[11] Maurice L. Rowntree, "Corporate Guidance and Church Government," *Studies in Quaker Thought and Practice*, Part II, London, 1936, p. 85. For further reference to the remarkable demonstrations of the method in 1920, see *Jordans, 1920*, the report of the International Conference of Young Friends.

It must not be supposed that the method herein described is used only for great matters, such as doctrinal and political positions. The method is successfully used also in relatively trivial matters and in these it is quite as thoroughly tested in view of the fact that such matters often arouse strong emotions. The method was admirably illustrated in one group which was divided on the question of the enlargement of a burial ground. The question arose because the old burial ground in the meeting house yard was filled. Strong sentiment was expressed, when the matter was first discussed, both for and against the enlargement. Those in favor of enlargement pointed out the fact that many families could not be given space for burial without increasing the size of the plot and that failure to give space was unfair discrimination between families. Those opposed to enlargement showed that the proposed action would limit the playground of the school, situated on the same grounds, and that it made the section less desirable for residences. It must be understood that this subject was one on which many felt deeply. Those whose loved ones were buried in the tiny space allotted could not consider anything in connection with it dispassionately and it is not surprising that they could not. Others were equally unable to consider dispassionately anything affecting the life of the school children. To them it was a matter of the interests of the dead against the interests of the living.

Since a decision seemed impossible on the first evening, the clerk made no minute and the problem was allowed to rest a month. It was not until six months later, however, that the question was settled and settled in a satisfactory manner. The strong emotional tone wore off, and several tempered their former statements, until at last it was decided to make a sufficient enlargement of the grounds to care for those now in membership and to make other arrangements for the future so that the question would not again arise. This small enlargement was made in such a way as to do no important harm to the playground, and all seemed to approve of the clerk's estimate of the sense of the meeting. Best of all the members did not feel that a weak compromise had been made, but rather that the very best plan had been followed.

The method of arriving at decisions on important or trivial matters which Friends have used for the greater part of three centuries has been well tested. In recent years a method greatly similar to the one described here has been used in the Fellowship of Reconciliation and by leaders' groups at student conferences. Though it sometimes fails and though it sometimes causes delay, we cannot but be impressed with its general success, when the basic principles are respected. It was just two hundred and seventy-five years ago that Edward Burrough exhorted Friends to pay close heed to these basic principles and the advice is still worth giving. Burrough asked Friends to proceed in their meetings, "not in the way of the world as a worldly assembly of men, by hot contests, by seeking to out-speak and overreach one another in discourse, as if it were . . . two sides violently striving for dominion in the way of carrying on some worldly interests for self-advantage." These are real dangers and the chief strength of the Quaker method has lain in a well organized effort to avoid them. What Friends have to teach about the conference method is the fact that even the search for truth is best conducted in a reverent, humble spirit, with quietness of mind, and with great patience.

# VI

## FRIENDS AND SOCIAL THINKING

### Clarence M. Case, Ph.D.
#### Professor of Sociology, University of Southern California

THE term "social thinking," as used in this chapter, means two things. One is the disposition to think about social conditions and social welfare. The other is the practice of thinking about these or other subjects in concert, though not necessarily in agreement, with other persons and groups. The one is social thinking because its subject-matter is social. The other is social thinking because it is done by interaction with one's associates, near or remote.

There are three factors which enter into social thinking. One is the practice of *uttering the truth,* in words or deeds. Another has to do with *influencing the attitudes of other persons* toward the truth, particularly with reference to social conditions and personal and social welfare. The third consists in *keeping the avenues open* by which truth may be freely expressed. It is the purpose of the present chapter to suggest something of the part the Society of Friends has played in these social processes, which, when equipped with a free public press and the other avenues of free speech, make public discussion, and hence public opinion, possible. Before such means of communication were invented and dedicated to democratic progress, there was possible merely that state of the social mind denoted by such terms as *"popular* sentiment" or *"popular* opinion," but no true *public* opinion. Popular sentiment means that similar emotional attitudes are prevalent among the populace, or people. Popular opinion means that an observer would find the same sort of private opinions expressed widely among the people. But *public* opinion can be attained only after the public discussion of common interests, such as is made possible by newspapers, political campaigns, forums, and radio broadcasting.

In seventeenth-century England, where the Quaker movement arose, there was no fully developed public opinion but much more of an approach to it than in many other parts of the world. It was in such a rurally scattered, relatively unorganized, social world that early Friends began their work. Under the circumstances one would not expect their methods to be identical with those we use today. There are many ways of uttering truth and influencing others to accept it, and they will be suggested in the following pages. Some of them are picturesque and even highly dramatic. The early Friends were gifted in the unlearned art of socially dramatizing their ideas and purposes. In other words, they acted them out effectively on the stage of social life in various ways.

All this acting and interacting on the part of the

people in any community is the social process
by which public opinion goes on. As Professor
Charles H. Cooley has shown most clearly,[1] public
opinion is not merely *agreement*. It consists just as
truly in social disagreement. It is a process of al-
ternating, or even simultaneous, agreement and
disagreement, going on constantly in the larger
group and the smaller groupings of which it is
made up. In such a process non-conformists and
dissenters play a very important part. Professor
Cooley stresses this, and utters it most finely in the
following sentence: "We shall be interested to find
whether Democrats or Republicans win the next
election; but how much more interesting it would
be to know what obscure group of non-conformers
is cherishing the idea that will prevail twenty years
from now."[2]

Obviously this applies with perfect aptness to
the Quakers and other dissenting sects of three
hundred years ago. In the infancy of their movement, which was at bottom a revolt against many
of the *mores,* or binding customs, of their day,
those early Friends and their like were cherishing
the idea of a world without slavery or war,—ideas
which outran their own day by many times twenty
years. They were preparing the way for the public
opinion, almost world opinion, of our own times,
against these ancient evils. One of the main objects
of this sketch is to show something of the spirit and

[1] In his books, *Social Organization* and *Social Process.*
[2] *Social Process,* p. 380.

methods by which the Quakers have stimulated and given direction to the social interaction of minds and the renovation of social values.

## I. UTTERING TRUTH

As for uttering the truth, the founder George Fox set a classic example. His *Journal* records, "While I was in that service [to a shoemaker and cattle dealer] I used in my dealings the word Verily, and it was a common saying among those that knew me, 'If George says verily, there is no altering him.'" This habit of his youth led to his frank and fearless practice of speaking the truth to authorities in later life, especially Oliver Cromwell, the Lord Protector of England. His half-dozen conferences with the Protector were primarily in behalf of persecuted Friends, but were quite cordial, and not always sought by Fox only. Yet this did not prevent the latter from recording in the *Journal* this remark on his own plain speaking:

Divers times, both in the time of the Long Parliament and of the Protector (so called) and of the Committee of Safety, when they proclaimed fasts, I was moved to write them, and tell them their fasts were like unto Jezebel's; for commonly, when they proclaimed fasts, there was some mischief contrived against us.

Stephen Grellett and other early Quaker ministers also stood before kings, among them the Czar of all the Russias, and uttered their messages boldly.

At a later time John Woolman, of New Jersey in this country, became equally famous for his gentle humility and faithful testimonies against practices which offended his tender conscience. In much lowliness and travail of spirit, he expostulated with the village inn-keeper for certain drunken revels which he had permitted, but now promised to abate. This was in Woolman's youth. A little later we see him refusing to finish a document which he had been engaged to draw up, because it included the sale of a slave. As his sense of the evil grew he felt it his duty to protest gently but firmly their exploitation of slaves to the Southern Quaker hosts who entertained him, his method being to ask permission to pay for the services rendered him by the slaves. Finally, in later years, he wore, with much embarrassment, an undyed suit of woolen homespun. This was his silent protest against what he looked upon as the luxury of some of the Philadelphia Quakers. It was his uttering the truth, as he saw it, without words, for, as Amelia Mott Gummere says in her *Introduction* to Woolman's *Journal,* "White hats were the fashion, and so completely were his motives misunderstood by some Friends, that for a time he could no longer preach. Nor was he at liberty to explain himself, feeling that this was a test of friendship."

In these two ways, the simple "Verily" of Fox in private conversation, and the prophetic testimony of himself and his fellow ministers in gov-

ernmental matters, we see illustrated the strong
tendency of the Quaker view of life to make of its
followers men and women much given to uttering
the truth in private conversation and public relations.

## II. INFLUENCING OTHERS

There are obviously two or three possible types
of response to the activities of other persons as
they impinge upon one's own interests. Aside from
those in which one actively co-operates, or main-
tains an attitude of indifferent neutrality, there
arise countless situations in which the choice lies
between submission and resistance. The last named
is the domain of conduct with which we are here
concerned, and it also in turn presents two aspects.
The first is the case where the subject resists or
repels the aggressions of others; the second is that
where he seeks to modify the conduct of others for
the purpose of promoting his own ideals. While
this often tends to merge into some form of coercion, such is not necessarily the case; since for
one who resists or seeks actively to control the conduct of others there are three, and if our analysis
is correct, only three methods of procedure. These
are persuasion, non-violent coercion, and violence.

Persuasion is that form of social action which
proceeds by means of *convincing* others of the
rightness or expediency of a given course of conduct. It may rely upon *argumentation,* which is the

recognized procedure to which the name is commonly applied; or it may seek to convince by suffering. Persuasion through suffering presents two types. The first is that so abundantly illustrated in passive resistance of the older, orthodox type. Perhaps nothing has stood out more prominently in accounts of the great passive resistants than their stress upon capacity and willingness to suffer. This suffering may be passively endured at the hands of others or self-inflicted, as in the modern instances known as the "hunger-strike." In either case the method is to produce in the mind of the one appealed to, who is here called the *subject,* a change of mental attitude without the use of coercion. In persuasion of the ordinary type he is convinced by a series of ideas or chain of reasoning. In persuasion by suffering it is done through the sight of distress which a word or simple act of resistance or consent on his own part would avert. When the suffering is self-inflicted for the express purpose of producing such a dilemma in the mind of the subject, as in the hunger-strike, this form of persuasion partakes of the nature of non-violent coercion, as explained below. But in the typical situation, where the suffering, while not self-originated, is passively endured, the beholder is persuaded and swerved from his course by a rush of admiration, gratitude, compassion, remorse, or other powerful emotion, while sometimes his hostile and threatening attitude is suddenly changed into one of active benevolence.[3] In a well-known sociological treatise the psychology of such situations is clearly formulated as follows: "A significant feature of sentiments and attitudes is inner tension and consequent tendency to mutation. Love changes into hate, or dislike is transformed into affection, or humility is replaced by self-assertion. This mutability is explained by the fact . . . that the sentiment-attitude is a complex of wishes and desires organized around a person or object. In this complex one motive—love, for example—is for a moment the dominant component. In this case components which tend to excite repulsion, hostility, and disgust are for the moment suppressed. With a change in the situation . . . these suppressed components are released and, gaining control, convert the system into the opposite sentiment, as hate." [4]

In the situation under discussion here, wherein the aggressor and moral-resistant confront each other, the mental movement is in the opposite direction, i.e., from hate to love; but it will be readily perceived that the process described is the same.

In meeting the opposition of hostile social forces the typical passive resistant has always shown himself strong to *suffer*. Therein are seen his "tokens of power," which have helped the laws of crowd

[3] All this has been concretely illustrated and fully explained in the present writer's earlier study, *Non-Violent Coercion: A Study in Methods of Social Pressure,* and the purpose here is simply to bring it under its proper category as essentially a form of persuasion.

[4] Park and Burgess, *Introduction to the Science of Sociology,* Chicago, 1921, p. 442.

psychology to work oftentimes in his favor. The courage and spectacular sufferings of the unresisting martyr impress tremendously the imagination of the crowd, producing "a startling image that fills and besets the mind." [5] In studying the religious persecutions of earlier passive resistants, the further fact must not be overlooked that the infliction of punishment and martyrdom is made a *public* affair by the persecuting authorities, in the very nature of the case. For they not only seek to impress the public mind but even depend upon the multitude to make the affair a success, although the people sometimes play a disappointing part from the point of view of the party of bigotry. Allard shows [6] how it was the practice during the early Christian persecutions to make the occasion "a spectacle and fête." The crowd gathered around the scene of torture, he finds, were "not only spectators, they were almost actors; the crowd filled then a role analogous to that of the chorus in the ancient tragedy; it was heard loudly expressing its sentiments; many times even, as if unconsciously, it fell to it to distinguish the various moral aspects of the drama which was being played before it." [7] A sort of social dialectic is thus set in motion by these "men of ardent conviction" who have always exercised the power to sway the multitude. [8] The spectacle of such suffering for a cause may lead

[5] Gustave Le Bon, *The Crowd*, London, 1903, p. 58.
[6] In his *Dix Leçons sur le Martyre*, pp. 332, 333.
[7] *Ibid.*
[8] Le Bon, *op. cit.*, p. 114.

even the persecutor to re-examine his own dogmas, if for no other purpose than to revel in their correctness. But re-examination admits new light, this modifies his view, and often the conquered becomes in the end the conqueror; for so effective is this social *indirection* of the passive resistant in forming public opinion that eventually persuasion may become the wiser policy on the part of government.

As a result of his striking devotion to principle, and his peculiarities, the image of the peace sectarian, as the symbol of a certain moral and social integrity, becomes impressed upon the public mind, figures in literature, art, and even in advertising,[9] and is of value to all concerned. It protects its bearers by capitalizing the past history of the sect for integrity and good will, and it inspires, through imitation, the same qualities in others. Thus, in the end, persecution, as "a short-cut to uniformity,"[10] goes down in defeat before the roundabout moral and social indirection of passive resistance.

It should be understood, however, that this applies only to those few instances where a passively suffering individual or group causes, by such means, an assailant to desist from his purpose, or advances an unpopular social policy toward final acceptance by society. It is to the process operating

[9] For example, the various commercial labels exploiting the picturesque images of the Shaker, Puritan, and Quaker.
[10] Cf. Edward A. Ross, *Social Psychology,* New York, 1908, Chap. XVII.

in such situations only that the term "persuasion through suffering" is herein applied.

The forms of non-violent coercion, as the present writer has called them, constitute the purest, most typical examples of *indirect* action in the field of social behavior. They are the strike, the boycott, and Gandhi's non-co-operation, which last-named is an extension of both the preceding to non-economic relations. One and the same principle underlies all these various manifestations, and that is a strategic recognition of the fundamental and indispensable importance of *co-operation* in every form and phase of associated life. More vital even than this is its recognition that this co-operation is necessarily more or less *voluntary* in every social situation and process, not excepting the grossest forms of exploitation, oppression, and tyranny. In the last analysis the victims always gild their own chains, even where they do not help to forge them. No people on earth ever yet had the dignity and self-control to refrain from gaping at the triumphal processions of its conquerors, or to refuse to validate the master's aggressions by accepting at his own valuation the titles and honors bestowed by his hand. India has come nearest to attaining this high moral level, but even there it is apparently no more than a passing phase. Nevertheless the method has been utilized to a greater or lesser degree, as witnessed by the fact that the strike and boycott are quite familiar instruments of coercive social pressure.

It is plain that persuasion and non-violent co-ercion must fall short of realizing the largest hopes of aroused and eager social crusaders, but it is still more clearly demonstrated that the methods of *violence* offer infinitely less of permanent good. But in the processes of democratic and progressive government, the excellencies of all these are blended, along with some of their evils which it may be entirely possible to eliminate. Therefore, in so far as the cause of the masses of disinherited men makes lasting headway, we cannot but believe that it will turn of necessity toward the democratic state as the one supreme adjuster of all conflicting interests, and as the only agency wherein the social gains of today may be permanently funded for the needs of tomorrow. For this reason those whose sympathies are with the masses in their struggles will look with approval on their all too feeble endeavors to gain control of government by the methods of public discussion and the ballot-box. This is the fruitful plan of constructive reform, by means of methods which no one can deprecate except selfish foes of democracy and of the general welfare. The proletariat have the numbers, if nothing else, to control the course of political action. All they lack is the political sagacity and the leadership to bring their voting power to bear in concert at the right point, and all things are theirs, within the limits of social possibility. The real trouble in the past has been that they have not enjoyed the support, even within the ranks of labor, of an organized public opinion, which is obviously the condition precedent to all effective legislation or other political action. The present rage for "direct action" by violent means is a misleading and fatal cry. The true direct action would be to get control of the State as the supreme agency of social justice, and the agency which is sure to have the last word in the end, because it represents nothing less than the dominant, effective, public will. If the exploited multitudes, everyone armed with his ballot, cannot find the wisdom and the patience to capture the State in times of ordered peace, they will never hold it captive long by violence and disorder.

The Friends were essentially democratic in their most fundamental religious convictions, and so naturally and inevitably democratic in social and political affairs. At the base lies their insistence on "the priesthood of all believers." This led in practice to the free, unprogrammed meeting for worship, where anyone might speak at will from the floor as well as the platform, out of the common ground of worshipful waiting in silence. Here the very nature of the service determined, as always, the nature of the building in which it was carried on. Thus one had the Roman Catholic service making the *altar* the architectural center of interest, and the elevation of the Host before the altar the climax of the service. The Protestant service and architecture centered in the pulpit, because the sermon was, and still is, the climax. The

Quakers, Dunkers, and similar groups, had no center architecturally speaking, and no climax of ritualistic character. Instead, there was a confrontation of the body of the house with rows of "facing seats" representing in themselves the essential oneness of the membership and the ministry. Thus the building and the congregation were on the democratic pattern. There was also *community* in this simple meditating company. That is to say, even as they sat in silence, as well as while speaking was in progress, they shared a common experience. As John Greenleaf Whittier puts it in his poem, *The Meeting,*

> "The strength of mutual purpose pleads
> More earnestly our common needs,
> And from the silence multiplied
> By these still forms on either side,
> The world that time and sense have known
> Falls off and leaves us God alone."

As the Quaker poet himself says in preceding lines, "this quiet shelter" was *not solitude.* It was, he says, much nearer to that state than the hills and shores, while at the same time truly social.

The same paradox appears in the manner of Friends in their business sessions. There the "sense of the Meeting," as discerned by the clerk, or presiding recorder, was the final decisive word, even after long and fervent debate. With no motions, and no voting of ayes and nays, no coercive parliamentary practices, one or two men, or women, might, and still may, be seen presiding over, but not ruling, the deliberations of an assembly numbering hundreds, even a thousand or so. It is made up of people who hold and express divergent views, yet acquiesce, without compulsion, in a common decision.

In all these things, including the public ministry itself, men and women were counted as of equal authority and power, thus making the spiritual democracy complete.

### III. KEEPING AVENUES OPEN

The Quakers are typical non-physical *resistants*. That is to say, they do not resist evil by physical violence, but they are noted for their resisting of political and social wrongs by *political* and *social* means. Historians have recognized that they have wielded an influence in English and American history out of proportion to their numbers, so that it is impossible to write the history of modern liberty and social reform without at the same time writing in part the history of the Society of Friends. The other peace sects, especially the Schwenckfelders, sometimes display this active tendency also, but their characteristic attitude has been that of *non*-resistance.

To take only a few instances of Quaker social and political activity: when it was realized that the denial by American colonial governments of the right of assembly could not be maintained except by actually exterminating the Quakers, there was nothing for the authorities to do but yield. This carried the right of exemption from tithes to the established church, a concession which, as we are told, "was won only by a long hard fight, but when it *was* won, it was won for everybody. . . . But," continues their biographer, Rufus M. Jones, "they did not stop with passive resistance to the tithe system. They laboured for three quarters of a century by every method known to their intelligence, or 'revealed to the mind of Truth' to get the tyranny abolished by statute." And, again, "as fast as they won their freedom they took up the fight on behalf of other peoples who were oppressed and hampered, and they proved to be good leaders of what seemed at the time 'lost causes' and 'forlorn hopes.'" In Maryland, in 1681, "Lord Baltimore announced to both houses that *'moved by the frequent clamours of the Quakers,'* [11] he was resolved henceforth to publish to the people the Proceedings of all the Assemblies." [12]

But perhaps the best illustration of the Quaker battle for English rights is to be found in a quaint work published in London in 1670. The title runs, "The People's ancient and just Liberties asserted in the Tryal of William Penn and William Mead, at the Sessions held at Old Bailey in London, etc." This little product of Quaker passive resistance describes in great detail the outrageous bullying of

[11] Italics mine.
[12] Rufus M. Jones, *The Quakers in the American Colonies,* London, 1911, pp. 153, 167, and 333.

the court, which was composed of the mayor, recorder, and an alderman of London, and records the fearless and able defense of Penn and Mead, who acted as their own attorneys. The prisoners were indicted under the charge of having "unlawfully and tumultuously assembled with Force and Arms." The evidence, however, showed simply that Penn had been preaching to an assemblage in the street near the meeting-house, from which the Quakers had been debarred by officers of the law. While they were thus peaceably engaged soldiers rushed upon and dispersed them, then trumped up the preposterous charge named in the indictment.

The defendants appealed to English charters and the common law, with an amazing knowledge of legal principles that probably not only mystified the learned court, but also irritated it.

The twelve "good men and true" were not so affected, however, and brought in a verdict to the effect that they found William Penn guilty of *preaching in the street,* and Mead not guilty of the same. The court promptly returned them to their cell without food, heat, or decent conveniences. For three days this continued, the court browbeating and raging incredibly at both defendants and jurymen. Penn and Mead exhorted them to stand firm for the liberty and rights of Englishmen, and the sturdy commoners stood true. The court was simply forced to accept the unique verdict, and the prisoners went free, but not until the recorder had declared himself in favor of a Spanish Inquisition in England for such fellows![13]

The important thing for the present account is that the Friends were not content to come off free from the charge of riotous assemblage. They took up the battle for the threatened liberties of the English people and spread the account of the trial before the public. The document contains also "A Rehearsal of the Material Parts of the Great Charter of England," the "Confirmation of the Charter and Liberties" of Edward I, and the "Sentence of the Clergy against the Breakers of the Articles above-mentioned," along with considerable other material designed to arouse the English people to their endangered rights. It was affirmed, in the *Introduction,* that there cannot "be any business wherein the People of England are more concerned than in that which relates to their Civil and Religious Liberties." The essential point is that this is not *non*-resistance. It does more than seek to triumph by passively suffering. It is a form of resistance that comes back to the fight and takes the aggressive, but always abhors the use of brute force in moral conflicts.

A special student of this phase of Quakerism

[13] It is interesting to note that a booklet on *The Trial of Penn and Mead* was announced (1921) by the Socialist *Appeal to Reason* in its "University in Print." The announcement pays the significant tribute: "Liberty, Equality and Fraternity have been preached through all time but it was left for William Penn, the Quaker, to come nearer establishing the ideal of this trinity than any other being called human before or since his day. Penn's defense in his trial . . . constitutes a mighty plea for the rights of men under Government."

remarks: "The protest of the Quakers against their arbitrary taxation by the Duke of York, in 1680, includes most of the arguments used by the Americans in 1776 against 'taxation without representation' and is an early Quaker movement in favor of independence nearly a century in advance of the event." [14]

The accession of William Penn lent to Quakerism that public turn which has contributed so much to give the Friends their unique place in the history of moral resistance.

Professor Cooley treats the problems of *right* and *conscience* as matters of "organization," and in his chapter on "The Social Aspect of Conscience" [15] he shows that the right is the *rational,* in a very profound sense, dealing with "the whole content of life, with instincts freighted with the inarticulate conclusions of a remote past, and with the unformulated inductions of individual experience." In this view, "conscience must be regarded as of a profounder rationality" than a superficial ratiocination, in case the two should chance to conflict, which is not usually the case. "The question of right and wrong," he continues, "as it presents itself to any particular mind, is, then, a question of the completest practicable organization of the impulses with which that mind finds itself compelled to deal. . . . It is useless to look for any

[14] Amelia Mott Gummere, *The Quaker in the Forum,* Philadelphia, 1910, p. 145.
[15] In Charles Horton Cooley, *Human Nature and the Social Order,* New York, 1902.

other or higher criterion of right than conscience. What is felt to be right *is* right; that is what the word means." Consequently, "for the individual considering his own conduct, his conscience is the only possible moral guide, and though it differ from that of everyone else, it is the only right there is for him; *to violate it is to commit moral suicide."*

Some today sigh for a dictator, which means someone to do their thinking and problem-solving for them. But that was tried, and failed, long before Mussolini and Hitler. The student of European history has read of the "benevolent despots," as they were called because they sincerely tried to benefit their people, yet insisted on doing everything themselves. Chief among them were Frederick I of Germany, Catherine II of Russia, and Franz Josef of Austria. The latter died bitterly disappointed at the "ingratitude" of his subjects. They were not ungrateful, however, but merely preferred to do things for themselves.

The present-day dictatorships of Italy and Germany are the natural outcome of certain acute situations following the World War. Moreover, they are doing, among incredibly evil deeds, certain good things which the people wanted to have done. But they have to face the problem of all dictatorial governments, namely, "Who can carry on the program when the original strong man is gone?" This is the more important because meanwhile the people have lost, instead of gained, in their ability to govern themselves.

## Friends and Social Thinking

In all dictatorships the avenues of free communication are ruthlessly cut off. Free speech, free peaceable assemblage, free press, free worship, free and open trial, free teaching, universal suffrage, the secret ballot, and many other priceless privileges are destroyed. In this, dictatorship is the enemy of democracy and freedom, regardless of all its good works. In that form of democracy known as a representative republic, such as the United States of America, it is supremely necessary that these great rights be kept unimpaired under all circumstances. This is absolutely necessary in order that the citizens may communicate freely with one another and with those who represent them in the affairs of government.

Foremost among the agencies of free communication are the newspaper and the radio broadcasting station. The well known fact that great metropolitan papers, or even great chains of them, have been turned by their wealthy owners into purely profit-seeking business is an ominous thing for democratic freedom. This is true because the thing called "news" is not the product of private enterprise, except certain ways of gathering it. The "news" itself is made by society. News is the history that is made, actually lived, every day by the people. Nobody owns it, or has any right to twist, mutilate, or misuse it. Yet that is done all the time by some newspapers as part of their deliberate policy. No informed and outspoken person will deny this, for it is admitted by experienced newspaper men themselves for the general run, although there are notable exceptions.

There are at least three reasons for this moral and social failure of the newspapers. *First,* the policy of "giving the readers what they want," which turns a newspaper into a sensational scandal sheet; *second,* the necessity of pleasing big advertisers or losing their patronage, which turns a newspaper into a suppressor of news; *third,* the attempt to color the news for personal, political, or class purposes, which degrades it to the level of a mere "organ." By this we mean that it is pretending to reflect the life of the world impartially, but is really practicing propaganda for special interests of private, rather than public, character.

This is a very great evil, for as the widely read publicist, Walter Lippmann, pointed out in his *Liberty and the News,* more important even than free expression of *opinion* is the right of newspaper readers to be given the undistorted facts on which alone any sound, worthwhile opinion can be based. In the light of their failure to treat the news fairly, and their suppression of certain public persons and issues at the expense of others, the outcry which certain newspapers have recently raised over supposed governmental encroachments on the "freedom of the press" is so inconsistent as to be absurd, as more honorable newspapers have pointed out. Freedom of the press in America has been injured by nothing except the fact that the mer-

cenary publishers of certain big papers have per-
sisted in running an enterprise, which is essentially
a social trust like the profession of medicine, teaching, and preaching, as if it were a purely private
business with no professional ethics to be maintained.

In view of the fact that the number of wave-
lengths is limited by nature, it is even more important that radio broadcasting be kept under
social control. Happily the Federal Government
has held them under close enough supervision to
insure fair practice. Moreover, the great broadcasting companies have thus far shown a very high
sense of responsibility to the public, particularly
in safeguarding freedom and fairness of utterance
at one and the same time. This is finely shown in
the pamphlet on *Political Broadcasts* printed by
the Columbia Broadcasting System, in 1936, in
which their dealings with the political parties are
set forth in a series of letters from their own files.

There is no problem more important for democratic social progress than the preservation of free
communication, especially through the newspaper,
the radio, the pulpit, the platform, including the
soap-box, and the teacher's rostrum.

We hear and speak a great deal about social
*goals* or objectives, but do not agree with the
widespread assumption that they are more important than *methods*. Exactly the contrary is true.
The most dangerous foe of free government and

true democracy is the man or woman who thinks that a good goal justifies any method found necessary to reach it. Strange to say, officers of the law have often been flagrant offenders in this way. One does not expect much else from the agents of modern despotism, or of the ancient world. But even in this country, dedicated to free institutions and democratic, non-violent methods, the law enforcement agencies have become so overzealous that twice, at least, they have been publicly condemned by some of the most outstanding legal authorities in America.

Such misdirected zeal from officials, along with atrocities and persecutions by night-riding mobs and self-styled "vigilantes" of various make-up, teach us that nothing is more important for democratic social progress than for all citizens to thoroughly understand the importance of the methods used under free government. Professor Edward A. Ross put this in most vivid form in his *Social Psychology,* published as long ago as 1908. He says, in words that every American would do well to memorize:

Seeing that no great wrong can long survive open discussion, we may characterize free speech, free assemblage, and free press as *the rights preservative of all rights.* Safeguard these fundamentals and the rest must come. This is why free government, although it is by no means the same thing as popular government, is usually the vestibule to it.

Those who violate these rights in their effort to reach even the finest goals, destroy the road that leads to all free goals, while those who mistakenly seek even unsound goals with most careful regard for these rights, leave the road open for the free seeking of all goals. Above all things the road of non-violent method, of peaceable persuasion by means of free speech, free assemblage, and free press, must be kept open to all without exception, no matter how mistaken in their ideals, or free government will perish. Those who attack these rights or deny them to others are the real enemies of democracy and social progress.

Early Friends played an heroic part in keeping open the avenues of free communication, such as free peaceable assemblage and free speech. Their successors have walked in the same tradition. They could not do otherwise and be real disciples of the Quaker tradition. But in very recent times Friends have not, apparently, made any special contribution along this line. A few of them, like their fellows of other faiths, have perhaps failed to hold with perfect clearness the supreme importance of "the rights preservative of all rights," in their fear of new forms of social radicalism. In the main, however, the Society of Friends will necessarily be found in the front rank of those who are now striving to save democratic freedom from the rising darkness of dictatorship in various parts of the world, though happily not in this land, except by a few undercover, night-riding movements.

During and immediately following the World

War, the American Friends Service Committee, following the lead of English Friends, entered upon a new line of work which was primarily the reconstruction of war-devastated lands, but which has a vital bearing on the question here before us. It creates a new avenue of communication between estranged nations and classes. While new it is also old, for it is the benevolent neutrality used by Irish Friends in the Civil War of 1798, and expounded so clearly by Dr. Thomas Hancock in his *Principles of Peace Exemplified,* published in 1826, and by the American Peace Society in 1843, under the title, *Hancock on Peace*.

The vital aspect of such benevolently active neutrality, for our present discussion, lies in the fact that the Friends who have engaged in it in World War France and Germany, revolutionary Spain, and those regions of Eastern United States torn by bitter industrial conflict, are really keeping open an avenue of reconciliation closed by bitter hatreds and deeds of violence. As they go about their impartial deeds of mercy and sacrifice, freely offered to both sides, they exemplify in living form the essential oneness of the humanity which has been sundered by the struggle. In so doing they keep open the avenues to communication and eventual reconciliation of the future. While enemies declare themselves utter aliens, those who do this service utter, even without words, the truth that both sides are one in ideal, and will eventually be one in fact.

### *Friends and Social Thinking*

Bitter partisans may deny their oneness for the
time being, but in order to remain truly human all
have to confess it in the end, the more so since they
see it acted out with compelling moral force before
their eyes from day to day.

# VII

## Marriage, the Family and the Community

### Robert H. Dann, A.M.

Assistant Professor of Economics and Sociology, Oregon State College

"In the salutation which we thus offer, we desire most heartily to associate the gracious partner of thy Throne. Feeling as we do that family life is the very corner stone of our political and social system, on the stability of which all depends, we rejoice exceedingly that thy subjects of every clime, looking toward the palace of their King, will see there an example such as they in their hearts know to be most worthy of imitation; husband and wife, parents and children knit together by the indissoluble bonds of family love."

—*An address from Friends in England to King George V* in 1910.

"Let there be famliies where love really rules within the family and in all external relationships, where a great purpose of social good permeates all, and with which the growing children become infected and inspired, where there is a natural happy sense of the divine Father's presence and where all is related to Him and springs forth from Him, and (then) these same characteristics must begin to show themselves throughout society."

—Henry T. Hodgkin's *The Christian Revolution,* p. 159.

### QUAKER FAMILY LIFE

A PART of the genius of George Fox was his ability to see the social implications of the religious position he took, and then to suggest ways by which a satisfactory adjustment of the two could be worked out. Often these adjustments led to a great deal of misunderstanding on the part of those who did not accept the religious position, but they met the needs of Friends who were willing to pay a price for what they held to be the truth. It is the purpose of this chapter to trace briefly some of the historical factors that are associated with the effects of the doctrine of the Inner Light in its application to marriage and the family. The material presented will be only suggestive of the mass that might be produced and which the writer hopes he may produce in fuller form at a later date.

Fox saw clearly that if he held strictly to his belief in the Inner Light, problems would arise in connection with the marriage ceremony and family life in general. A Friend could not be married by a priest; men could not dominate family life; women could not be despised as inferior; children had real claims on their elders and made real contributions to the life of the group. The family was an essential part of society, being molded by it and in turn having a good deal to do with the molding of Society; the whole needed definite spiritual motivation to secure the maximum benefit to the individual and to society.

Historically in the Christian era the control of the church over the marriage rites and, through them, over the family has passed through a slow development. In the first stage the new Christian Bishops or Priests were the invited guests at a civil ceremony, later the priest was the invited participant and acting orator at the ceremony frequently held on the steps of the church where he led the ofttimes timid couple in their responses; and, lastly, the marriage could only be accomplished under the direction of the priest. When so performed it became a sacrament symbolical of the relationship wedding Christ to His church. When Martin Luther broke from the church, he also broke from this sacramental marriage and returned to the older civil ceremony. In addition to this there was what was known as Common Law Marriage. It was used frequently among the poorer people. This form of marriage depended for its validity on a public demonstration of the fact that, in time, carried all the aspects of legality. George Fox must have been aware of this history. As late as 1678, he wrote to Richard Richardson, a Friend and schoolmaster in London, asking him to search all "libraries concerning marriage."[1] His reply dated August 10, 1679, reported that the ancient Jews, Gentiles, and early Christians all considered marriage to be a secular rather than a sacred rite.[2]

In the first place, the attitude of Fox toward the church itself made necessary some adjustment. There is a caustic statement from him under date of 1669 in which he implies that the priests "who have, some of them, the rough hands of Esau, and fists of wickedness, and who have had their hands

[1] Letter of Fox to Richardson, copied in *Journal of Friends Historical Society,* Vol. I, p. 62.
[2] An old copy of the original reply is in the Library, Friends House, London.

dipped in the blood of our brethren in New England," [3] and who, he goes on to relate, have been the cause of banishments, imprisonments, and much ill treatment of Friends, are not, in his opinion, fit agents of God to join man and woman together in matrimony. Friends' marriages, performed without priest or bishop, were considered illegal and children of such marriages, illegitimate. In the record of the visitation of the Bishop of Chester for the year 1665, we find references such as the following: "Against John Eaton and his pretended wife, Robert Taylor and his pretended wife, John Minshell and his pretended wife, Samuel Naylor and his pretended wife, Thomas Bretton and his pretended wife, Quakers, for being unlawfully wedded." [4]

In the *American Extracts* [5] under the heading *Ancient Testimonies,* there is a reference to the legality of the Friendly marriage procedure. It runs as follows: "Divers instances have been adjudged good in law though they were not solemnized by Priests, for brevity we omit, and shall only mention a Cause which our honorable Friend and Elder Brother, George Fox, in his journal said was tried in the assizes at Nottingham in the year 1661. The case was thus—'Some years before, two Friends were married among Friends and lived

[3] *The Epistles of George Fox,* p. 276.
[4] *Journal of Friends Historical Society,* Vol. III, p. 28.
[5] This is a hand-written volume of Advices given from Time to Time by the Yearly Meetings of Friends for Pennsylvania and New Jersey.—1760. It is in the library at Haverford College.

together as Man and Wife, about two years. The man died leaving his wife with Child, and an Estate in Copy-Hold Lands, when the Woman was delivered, the Jury presented the Child Heir, who was accordingly admitted, afterwards one that was near of Kin to the childs father, brought that suit thereby intending to deprive the child of the inheritance, and to effect this he would prove the Child Illegitimate, alleging the Marriage was not according to Law. After the Counsel on both sides had been pleading, Judge Archer directed the Jury to find the Child Heir, which they did accordingly.' By this we may understand, how far we are justified in the Method of consummating our Marriages by mutual promises, which are made in much awe and reverence in the Presence and audience of God's People at their religious assemblies: but it is understood that though we are present at such Solemnities, yet we marry none but are witnesses thereto as any other Spectator may be." [6] The quotation goes on to warn Friends that they need not fear for the legality of their marriage nor the legitimacy of their children.

In order to secure for the proposed substitute form of marriage not only legality but also a degree of respectability that would at least avoid the odium so often attached to the Common Law Marriage as a marriage of convenience, Friends took great pains to establish certain rules that would, at least in a measure, gain this desired end. We find

[6] *American Extracts,* now in Haverford Library.

them concerned as to the matter of adequate consent, for those contemplating marriage, from their parents or guardians. In one place in the *American Extracts* under date of 1694, we find this: "And it hath been the advice of our Friends as may be seen in the Yearly Meeting Epistle from London 1691 amongst many other weighty things, thus expressed, that 'great care be taken about marriages for the Consent of Parents.'"[7] Again, a statement such as this from an old record in Scotland "and let parents on both sides know the minds of each other about portions before their children make any promise. In the case of marrying—they make their minds known one to the other."[8]

This point of knowing beforehand adequately what their wishes were in regard to marriage was also emphasized by the process known as "Passing Meeting." It involved a series of public announcements on the part of the individuals most concerned of their intentions to marry. There were many stages in the process, but in general three things stood out that may have some bearing on the quality of their family life; a period of hesitation of at least a month; an investigation by a committee of Friends to be of help and assistance to those contemplating marriage and thirdly, if the marriage seemed fitting, a committee would then be appointed to plan for and to supervise the wedding. The ceremony would usually take place in

[7] *American Extracts,* now in Haverford Library.
[8] *Journal of the Friends Historical Society,* Vol. VIII, p. 69.

conjunction with a meeting for worship. At an appropriate time during the meeting, the couple in question would arise, take each other by the hand and simply make their declarations. The form of expression that became most acceptable was this "I [name of the man] take thee [name of the woman] to be my wife, promising, with the Lord's assistance, to be unto thee a loving and faithful husband until death separate us." There are some more interesting statements than this that were used by Friends in the early days with an occasional "promise to obey" on the part of the woman; this latter became obsolete as time passed. For example, in the case of Middleton-Mollison, the bridegroom said, "My Friends and all of you that are here present, you are my witnesses this day that I do solemnly and in the fear of God take this, my friend, Jane Mollison, to be my wife, in which I do promise by this Grace to be her loving and faithful husband until death separate us." And the bride said, "Friends and people who I desire to be my witnesses that in fear of God, I take this, my friend, Joshua Middleton, to be my husband and do promise by the Lord's assistance to be a faithful, dutiful, and submissive wife, until it shall please the Lord, by death, to separate us." [9] Following this statement, the meeting would conclude when the bride and groom publicly signed a certificate that certified their having been married. As many Friends of those

[9] *Journal of the Friends Historical Society,* Vol. XIV, p. 136.

present at the meeting as cared to do so would sign their names to the certificate. In the case cited above there were ninety-eight such signatories, including William Penn. This certificate was cherished by the family as being the evidence of their marriage. This ceremony was recorded carefully in the books of the Monthly Meeting, where it became the permanent record. Here the public statement was made before the couple began living together, whereas in Common Law Marriage there was involved a public recognition made after the individuals involved had been living together for some time.

To insure a proper ordering of their family life we find Friends showing concern for many details. Rules were developed to meet situations as they arose. True, as we shall see, the rules became the rulers and Friends became enslaved by them. There are repeated references and rulings as to the inadvisability of marriage to one near of kin. A study of the Disciplines shows that though the degree of consanguinity permitted was not fixed beyond possible changes, there was a great deal of discussion as to what was the proper procedure. A quotation from the *American Extracts* under date of 1685 says that, "Friends of Chester Quarterly Meeting desired to have the judgment of this meeting whether it be allowable for the Father and the Son to marry two sisters; the meeting, well weighing the same, did give it as their present sense that such marriages ought to be discountenanced."

In a letter included in the *American Extracts* from Thomas Ellwood, written in 1706, he says, "It seems to me not to be lawful amongst any, much less amongst Friends, for a man to marry his wife's first or second cousin." He referred to Leviticus for his support where it suggested affinity and consanguinity to be identical. In this same letter Ellwood tells how he served on a committee of the Yearly Meeting to advise with one of the Suffolk Monthly Meetings in a case where a Friend did propose marriage with "his former wife's Brother's daughter." He says that he secured a "unanimous sense of the committee that the parties should be encouraged to discharge each other."

There was equal concern that remarriage be not too hasty. At one time it was suggested that no remarriage should take place before nine or ten months had passed. Very early remarriage was common in colonial days. Hidden in the records of one meeting, is a story concerning a woman Friend whose husband, a sea captain, had been long overdue from the Orient, so much so that many thought him lost at sea. The wife or widow proposed remarriage; but the meeting advised against remarriage, fearing the former husband might appear. The woman finally remarried outside the Society.

At their weddings, Friends were advised against much show and worldliness. Some of the accounts of marriages indicate that fine clothes and an abundance of tasty foods were not uncommon. The fact that there are frequent references to these practices, by way of constraint, in the Disciplines and Epistles would indicate their existence in the practice of some Friends at least.

Many Friends suffered persecution and imprisonment for adherence to the new rules. They resented any appearance of fickleness. In an Epistle of 1669—George Fox said, "And all men that hunts after women, from woman to woman; and also women, whose affections runs sometimes after one man, and soon after another, and so hold one another in affection, and so draws out the affections one of another, and after a while leave one another, and go to others, and then do the same things more; these doings are more like Sodom than Saints, and is not of God's own moving . . . , for marriage is God's ordinance." There are stories in the records of how individuals, both men and women, were asked as to their intentions one toward the other by the Meeting. One case in 1676 says, "Easter Kerke was inquired of by Friends how things were betwixt her and Francis Tomlinson—it being understood that she had kept company with him for long, and then cast him off." She explained that he had often spoken his mind toward her, but she had told him she did not think well of it, but she had not denied him " 'til of late," and he was much disturbed. The meeting "exhorted her to be more careful hereafter." There are many other rules referred to in the disciplines that were designed to give a great security, if not sacredness, to the Quaker family.

It was probably inevitable that when the fire of persecution subsided and the strain of being a Quaker was lifted, the prevailing attitude of mind became an inward searching rather than an outward experimentation. Following the recognition of their rights in the Act of Toleration in 1689, decided changes of practice and behavior appear in the Society. It is our interest here to see how this affected family life. We find the rules, which had been developed as aids, became standards for measurement.

Attention should be called to the concern which grew up in regard to marrying those who were not members of the Society or marrying not according to the rules. The Disciplines and literature of the period are replete with references to the procedure that ended in disownment. Any man or woman who married an individual not a member of the Society of Friends or who was not married according to their custom, but by a priest, was to be proceeded against. Unless satisfactory explanation or adjustment was made, such Friends were dropped from membership. It has often been pointed out that during a long period of years, there were so many disownments that the Society lost its power and standing in the community.

A farsighted but anonymous individual in 1858 offered a prize of one hundred guineas for the best essay that would explain why the Society of

Friends had not alone failed to grow in numbers with the expanding population in England, but had lost prestige and power. John Stevenson Rowntree in his book *Quakerism, Past and Present,* the first prize essay, called attention to a great many causes for this decline. In his chapter on "Mixed Marriages" he calls attention to the fact that early Friends recognized the difficulty any small group would have that desired its younger members to marry among its membership. In the early days in Pennsylvania and New Jersey Friends were sufficiently numerous to avoid the pinch of this situation, but as the population grew in numbers faster than the Society, the cases of infraction of the rules became more numerous. He quotes from the *Journal* of Samuel Bownas, written in 1728, "There were always some who broke the rules, but a suitable acknowledgment was made and all parties were satisfied." He called attention to the increasing tendency to enforce the discipline and to an "increasing reliance on the final exercise of the discipline as a preventive to these marriages." It becomes evident, as he proceeds, that the devices used by Friends in an earlier day to dignify and give legality to their marriages, were not designed to meet the demands of a more settled society at a much later date. What we now call a "culture lag" had appeared. In defense of this policy, it should be said that, in the first instance at least, the real concern was not that the marriage was wrong and that the offending individual should express his regrets for marrying, but that the way in which the marriage was carried out had brought "dishonor on Truth." [10]

A further reference to Rowntree will give a few figures. He examined the records of numerous monthly meetings and concluded that in those meetings located near York, in England, one-third of those marrying were disowned. He used this sample as a basis for concluding "that of the 4499 marriages solemnized in Friends meeting houses, representing 9889 persons between the years 1800 and 1855, about half that number will have married contrary to the Society's regulation; and in consequence, has been disowned." He is assuming here that all those young Friends getting married contrary to rule were married in the meeting-house, a condition not at all likely. He concluded,

[10] An instance of disownment.

#### EDWARD WHITEHOUSE DENIAL

Whereas Edward Whitehouse of Dover hath for many years made a large profession of the Blessed Truth with us the people commonly Called Quakers but through unwatchfulness hath suffered his mind to wander from the way thereof into a Liberty which truth allows not of: so as to keep Company with a woman in order to marriage that is not of our profession altho we have Laboured with him in Love in the Early proceedings thereof to reclaim him yet he would not harken to our Christian Council and advice therein but hath proceeded to the accomplishing of his 2nd marriage Contrary to the good orders Established amongst Friends. These therefor are to Certifie whom it may Concern that we do disown and deny his evil deeds and him and that we have no unity with him until he Returns from the Evil of his ways by unfained repentance and that he may do so is the sincear desire of our Lord for him . . .

Signed in and on behalf and by order of our monthly meeting held at Dover by adjournment from the 20th to the 25th day of the 11th m. 1732/3

Timothy Robinson
Ebenezer Varney
John Canne
John Trombly

This friend was later reunited with the meeting.

"We make no apology for occupying so much space with this portion of our subject, for it will be at once seen that the disownment of four thousand adult members just at that period of life when most likely to add to the strength of the Society more than explains its numerical diminution during the present century." Even during the period of the most rigorous application of the disownment rules, which were in some cases applied to parents who aided or consented to such marriage as brought "dishonor on Truth," the number of such marriages quite naturally increased.

The change of policy can be traced through the Yearly Meeting minutes of this period. It gradually came and ended in a recognition of the marriage of any member of the Society to whomever he might choose, and the abolition of the disownment process. The change was made with relatively little difficulty. It came first in London Yearly Meeting, in the year 1858, the proposition coming up from Yorkshire Quarterly Meeting, the home of John Stevenson Rowntree to whose essay reference has been made, then in Race Street Yearly Meeting of Philadelphia in 1865 in a proposition from Philadelphia Quarterly Meeting, and at Arch Street Yearly Meeting of the same city in the year 1881.

There was surprisingly little comment in the various periodicals published at this time concerning this drastic change in a procedure that had become well entrenched and the enforcement of which had been accompanied by many strained family ties. One comment in *The Friend*,[11] says, "The marriage rules as altered by our late Yearly Meeting may to some appear an improvement, but time can alone determine their value, which, therefore, for the present must be considered problematical." This indicates flexiblity among Friends even after a century or more of rigid regulation.

The journals of Friends reveal some remarkable illustrations of parental understanding of children and their ways. In this connection the letter of advice from Francis Howgill to his daughter is classic.[12] "The Advice of Thomas Dann to his children" who were about to be inoculated against the smallpox, shows an understanding and wisdom in dealing with youth.[13]

Such queries as the following held before Friends their responsibilities. "Do your young people receive the loving care of the meeting, and are they brought under such influences as tend to promote their religious life and to give them an understanding of the principles and practices of minds?"[14]

An Epistle from London Yearly Meeting in 1723, entitled "An Epistle of Caution and advice to Parents Recommending a Goodly Case for the

---

[11] *The Friend*, Philadelphia, 3:28:1881.
[12] *Life of Francis Howgill,* James Backhouse, p. 85.
[13] *Bulletin of Friends Historical Association*, Vol. 23-1, p. 246.
[14] The Queries comprised questions asked of members and meetings that suggested forms of behavior held to be consistent with the fundamental positions of Friends. They varied from time to time as the social scene changed, and today have a bearing on the social and religious problems of our age.

Educating their Children in a Christian Conversation," made specific suggestion as to how this might be achieved. It is urged that parents "tell their Children of their own experiences and what God hath done for their Souls: for it is very often seen that the good Impressions that children receive in their tender years from their parents are not easily worn out."

The practice of family visiting was and still is held to be a very important responsibility of Friends. Often, where Friends were not performing the function freely, they were urged to appoint suitable Friends to visit. It was suggested that if such Friends could not be found in a particular meeting, some members from other meetings should be requested to perform this service. It was felt to be so important that the *American Extracts* reports that there were "several testimonies borne by experienced Friends to EXITE such as have not performed that service to undertake it and to encourage others to be more frequent in the exercise thereof." The motive for much of this visiting was often, according to the Extracts for 1747, to "prevent many growing inconveniences and customs amongst us, which it may be difficult guarding against in a more public manner"; even so, the custom has much to commend it. In the darker days it was used to hold or maintain the status quo, but this is not the necessary and only result of such a practice. Some of the finest moments in the life of many families doubtless came during such visitations, and probably some of the weakest also sprang from this source when the visiting was of a blundering sort and the motives of the visitor open to question.

The education of their children suited to the needs of their day was another concern of Friends. George Fox himself encouraged the education of girls. Some of the earliest enterprises of Friends were their schools. A query from New England dated 1785, after some questions about the care of the poor, asks, "Do their children freely partake of learning to fit them for business, and are they and other Friends' children placed among Friends?" There are still meetings that take this responsibility seriously and provide advanced education in Friends schools, where the family cannot afford it.

The belief that reading makes an impression on one's thinking and behavior, caused Friends to show considerable concern for the type of reading matter that was available. A Query dated 1806, asks, "Are Friends careful to bring those under their direction . . . in frequent reading of the Holy Scriptures and to restrain them from reading pernicious books and from the corrupt conversation of the world?" It is not surprising, therefore, that they undertook to publish material designed for their members, both young and old. A casual survey of some of their publications will show that they were not intended merely as newspapers for the Society, but provided topics for study and dis-

cussion of a very general nature. The constant publication and re-publication of journals of ancient
Friends was motivated by this same desire to supply ample and proper reading matter.

Friends have consistently urged the need for
careful and frequent reading of the Scriptures
with their families and those under their care. In a
great many homes, not alone the immediate members of the family, but all the helpers in the house
and on the grounds were assembled at least once
a day for a period of solemn and reverent reading
and waiting. This practice has claimed the concern of Friends in each generation, and at times
they have been required to report to the meeting,
their "degree of faithfulness." In view of the very
liberal attitude of early Friends toward the Scripture, this concern is all the more striking. The part
played in the development of adult attitudes and
mature personality by such practices cannot be
measured. It produced a knowledge of the Bible,
especially the choice parts suited to frequent quotation; it gave an acquaintance with and practice in
prayer and, perhaps as important a fact as any,
it supplied a basis for a religious and spiritually
motivated group solidarity that is a valuable part
of family life.

The Queries give an insight into the problem
of suitable recreation as they reflect the attitude
of Friends as well as the current social vices.
Friends were never forbidden to play the "risky
games" but were warned of the dangers and ad-

vised to refrain. Open disregard might result in a public rebuke in Monthly Meeting or at the hands of a committee. The supervision of social life did eliminate a freedom in the development of arts and skills that we now believe add to the development of personality. Abuses that arise are the evils to guard against rather than the arts or pleasures themselves.

A modern Query asks, "Do you choose those recreations which will strengthen your physical, mental and spiritual life, and avoid those that may prove a hinderance to yourselves and others; and do you so live that spiritual growth, family life, the interests of the Church, and public welfare may have their due share of your time and thought?" [15]

Friends early became famous for their ability in business. They were good business men. The farmers amongst them were good farmers. They undertook to care for the needs of all their members but strove to educate and train all of them to be self-supporting. A family in financial difficulty was sure to get help from the meeting. A member, undertaking a new business venture, would ask the advice of the meeting. Friends were urged not to become involved in business beyond their ability to manage. Young people were trained, often in the business of a Friend, in efficiency, honesty, frugality, and diligence.

The effect of this care in economic matters was to produce a relatively wealthy group. Such a

[15] *Faith and Practice,* Philadelphia, 1935.

friend of the Friends as Thomas Clarkson, writing at the beginning of the nineteenth century, after a somewhat flattering description of the Quaker character, calls attention to some "Imperfect Traits." [16] He enumerates, "The next trait is that of a money-getting spirit—probability of the truth of this trait is examined—an undue eagerness after money not unlikely to be often the result of the frugal and commercial habits of the society—but not to the extent, as insisted on by the world— this eagerness, wherever it exists, seldom chargeable with avarice." In the second section of the chapter he calls attention to some "Practicable methods suggested for its extirpation that would not appear inconsistent with the religion they confess." He knowingly suggests several ways in which this might be effected; such as, setting a certain sum as the maximum family income, which when attained should be a signal for retirement from business or that gifts to charity should be increased to such an extent as to keep down the tendency to excessive family expenditures. An advice from London in 1845 says, "Those who have acquired a competency are to watch the proper period at which they may withdraw from the cares of business and when disengaged to beware how they employ their property in investments which may involve a new care and anxiety. Not to trust uncertain riches nor hold out to their chil-

---

[16] Clarkson's *Portraiture of Quakerism*, Vol. III, Ch. 13. The heading.

dren expectation of ease and abundance but fix
their hope on that which is substantial and eternal."

John Stevenson Rowntree, in a pamphlet published in the nineties, called attention to the fact
that certain factors in society had forced Friends
into closed groups. They lived very much to themselves, married among their own members, were
educated in their own schools, made their living
working with or for members of the society, and
married according to the respected order. The
whole life of the group was organized for it from
birth to death. He shows that in the nineteenth
century conditions outside the Society had so
changed as to make this isolation impossible and
unnecessary. Politics, business, law, education,
marriage laws had all dropped the barriers that
formerly caused Friends to develop their closed
group. There was no longer any justification for
the special appellation of a "Peculiar People."
The conditions in the twentieth century have so
completely broken down the isolation that we find
Friends exhibiting evidences of nervousness and
embarrassment as they face a world that is anxious
to receive them. In a measure, the problems of
the family have been increased by this very fact.
The forms and scope of business have spread the
interests of Friends to more expansive concerns
and larger territory. The possibility of entering
the legal profession and politics, as well as freedom to enter a college without the necessity of
a preliminary religious inquisition as was formerly

required in England, and many similar facts have altered the modern situation.

The brochure from the joint committee of the Philadelphia Yearly Meetings recognizes the problems that the present social situation has forced upon them. The title "Home Building" is suggestively constructive: "The purpose of this paper is to urge that the building of homes be as carefully planned as the building of houses. Of course the building of a house is recognized as a serious matter. No one would think of investing much capital in one without the expert advice of an architect as a guide. How much more delicate is the structure of a successful and permanent home!"

"1. Physical fitness is of great importance. We advise that both man and woman undergo an adequate physical examination in order that any serious physical handicaps be early discovered and, if possible, corrected. There are certain diseases which are not only contagious but which may seriously affect the lives of the next generation.

"2. Much has been written on sex and our proper attitude toward it. We suggest frank discussion in the light of the modern psychological viewpoint. Literature is available which covers the matter far more fully than this paper can. The general principle involved seems to be that no natural function of the body should be regarded with embarrassment by those who are planning to merge their personalities in the greatest of life's adventures. Physical union and spiritual union are complementary parts of any true marriage.

"3. Social equality between man and wife is of great value. It often occurs however that people fall in love who come from circles which do not have social contact . . . if the families cannot be reconciled the cost should be counted and the couple should decide either to give up their plans or to build a solidarity between themselves in spite of the handicap. If the social differences are in education let the gap be closed as far as possible through the steady pursuit of education . . . reading, or actual attendance at school. If the social gap is a racial one it might be necessary for one of the couple to make a serious sacrifice in the interests of a solid home.

"4. Common ethical ideals are important. One of the great necessities of mutual happiness is mutual trust and confidence. Man and wife must be able to depend upon each other. This is something that engaged couples can build toward very definitely . . . Love eventually breaks down where mutual respect is lacking. 'Two minds with but a single thought' is not an idle dream; it is a happiness obtained by two personalities who have without reservation opened themselves to each other, having kept no secrets.

"5. Mutual interests seem to be a great power for binding souls together though it is quite possible for two people who have no common interests to fall in love with each other. Many think that here is the root of most unhappy marriages:—physical attraction, without the backing of common interests. Convergence of minds is the logical path to happiness and can be the result of conscious planning. . . . There are people happily married in spite of divergence of interests but they base their married life upon things they do have in common.

"6. Financial provision must be made for meeting the expenses of the home. It is a very unfortunate thing when finances delay marriage beyond a reasonable time. For those who have sufficient income to warrant marriage some definite budget should be worked out, life insurance purchased and economy practiced. . . .

"7. Religious fellowship has often been stressed. It seems evident that people with basically similar philosophies of life are more likely to grow closer to each other than those without a common religious outlook.

"It would seem advisable for people who intend to live their lives together to clarify their religious ideas by open comparison in search for what they have in common, and then to attempt to get together in their religious thinking. Religion is a thing of the depths of personality. Love and religion have much in common and can strengthen each other greatly. Love without religion lacks its most loyal ally.

"These suggestions have their origin in a plainly

observable fact. While many people rush into matrimony with the comforting thought of marriages being made in Heaven, we can see that happy homes do not happen by chance. When two people consciously and constantly dedicate themselves to the task they are certain to achieve a happy home."

The purpose of this historical and sociological discussion has been to lay the foundation for a few conclusions that might be drawn. The following points stand out clearly: First, that woman is man's equal both from a theological, as well as a social point of view. No man has a right to demand of a woman obedience which he is not willing to give her. The kind of life he is expected to live does not require such assertions of male superiority nor such binding statements as the usual ceremony required. It has been expected that Friends, married to Friends, would stay together through "sickness and health," and that financial reverses should not break their faith in each other.

This elevation of woman to her rightful place as an equal with man was not based upon New Testament ideas, especially not upon Pauline traditions, but could be shown to be a reasonably reliable bit of human experience; Jesus recognized it and any right-living person would accept it. The Puritans, in accepting the Biblical standard, found themselves, and we would like to believe in some cases at least reluctantly, forced to establish a relationship of superiority and inferiority between men and women. If any Friend opposed woman suffrage, it had to be on some other grounds than those of inequality and values as persons.

Second, the community was very much interested in the success of marriage among its members. Weddings were not rushed into blindly, love at first sight was not synonymous with marriage in the morning. Enough time was required for a degree of maturity of affection to appear. There was enough publicity to test the genuineness of the betrothal. It could never be claimed that this same degree of care and concern might not produce an effect just the opposite of that desired, and perhaps cause some who have made public their love to fear a retreat even though they might recognize its essential wisdom. This concern shows the community's interest in marriage. The committees appointed to investigate the situation were not committees of criticism and examination, but of assistance and advice in starting the married career. One of the interesting by-products of this was the establishment of various funds that were designed to assist young people contemplating marriage to work out their financial problems. In England today there is a very active fund that offers considerable financial support to young men and women Friends under certain circumstances, who are contemplating marriage. The fund was established during the early decades of the nineteenth century, and is known as the Marriage-Portion fund. This fund constantly advertises its service in the British Quaker periodicals. There were other funds established that offered financial assistance to those who were contemplating marriage. There is no doubt but that at times this sort of interference became objectionable; but, on the whole, it would appear to be a very suitable concern of the elders and of the community. Mating may be purely a biological affair, but marriage and the family are social. The community is inevitably involved in every marriage, and no marriage can be entirely divorced from the community.

A third factor stands out clearly in connection with the rearing of children. Children were the natural outcome of marriage, and the responsibility for their education and care was essentially a responsibility of the community. No family, or very few, could possibly undertake this task alone, but the welfare of the community depended on the successful fulfillment of the process. The concern was not that children be raised to be religious, not that they be good business men or housewives, but that they realize that life is a well-rounded whole, so that religion and business can never be separated from any other part of life. This study also justifies the conclusion that at times a whole group must be prepared to face the consequences of law violation when the current law interferes with their loyalty to a principle that seems to them to be of lasting value. The result of the protest of early Friends has secured the right to be married according to any well-established order, free from the dictation of a dominating group, but still within the supervision of society at large.

# VIII

## THE ECONOMIC LIFE

### David E. Henley, Ph.D.

Professor of Economics and Sociology, Whittier College

PERSONAL spiritual experience and practical social behavior are inseparable halves of one way of life, for the Quaker. A statement of the meaning this has for the social order would be a genuine service to Friends as well as to others. However, this story cannot be written yet. All one can do is to indicate some factors or elements that enter into that message. The development of this new "testimony" is now taking place.

As indicated below, Friends have applied their principles to these practical problems in other days. It is possible that they may succeed once more. In the days when dishonesty prevailed in personal business, they were embarrassed by the success which came to them through application of their religious teachings in trade. They applied honesty and integrity when these were not the rule. When church, trade, and state were dominated by dogma, bigotry, exploitation, and intolerance the Quakers revolted against the moral conduct and standards of the times. For their honesty and mercy as much as for their tolerance and independence they were viewed with suspicion and alarm.

## The Economic Life

Today the Society of Friends is in a new state of flux and change. After a quiescent period it is trying once more to dream new dreams, to resolve new inconsistencies, to follow the "Light Within" into newly lighted areas of human behavior. New inconsistencies coming to light create new problems. New attitudes, new passions, and new hopes are appearing among those individuals who are more sensitive to the "Light." Those who are not too old, or too deeply involved in old practices, are responding to the leadership of these new Quakers. But where the movement will go or when it will end is a question that must be left for the future historian to answer.

Are there here—as in Fox, Penn, Bright, and Woolman—the elements for another spiritual revolution? Can the old institution, with an old name and an old set of attitudes and practices be revitalized yet once again? Can this old wineskin carry new wine still another time? The parts for the making of such a spiritual-social reformation may be here but the "odds" seem to be against the mass of the Society rising to the situation. The present scene suggests that the institution is now too firmly tied down, with too many vested interests and too many institutional values and respectabilities. Dr. Belasco's remark about the church at the time of the rise of the Quakers may apply to these Quakers themselves today: "The churches, far from being adventurers into truth, fell from being interpreters to caretakers." Friends today are too accustomed to the sight of social and economic sin and too comfortable once more to champion the cause of the despised poor and disinherited. An internal revolution will have to take place in the life of the Society before there is any "revolution of brotherly love." Quaker principles have, still, an effective and imperative challenge to materialism, imperialism, exploitation, and violence. The question is that of a revived spiritual vitality,—whether this Truth can "come alive and march again." This is a question of the life of the Society itself. For without consistency in practical life Quakerism dies, since that is a central and integrating factor of the spiritual life of the Society.

### SHARING THE GOOD LIFE—THE DILEMMA!

The problem of "distribution" in economics is the problem of sharing opportunities, controls, and productive tasks—dividing economic rewards among the classes of income-receivers. Production effectively organized to secure an adequate supply of goods and services must accompany a just and humane system for apportioning the total income. Economists are interested, not in selling cabbages and potatoes, but in distributing opportunity, security, health, education, leisure, freedom, and the joy of creative participation.

Quakerism implies that a good system of distribution would be one which helped to *conserve men* as well as natural resources and capital. It says that the human factor must be taken into account, that if the present system cannot consider this more adequately than in the past then it will commit social suicide and be replaced by a social order which can consider the personal elements of civilization. In essence, the Quaker says, "I insist on my right to examine social conduct in the light of the Sermon on the Mount and to help build a spiritual fellowship. Both for the good of my own soul and for that of my fellowmen I must help come to grips with the pagan elements of this present order, help rebuild it, make it more tolerable for my fellowmen." Quakerism teaches that any civilization, if it is to become permanent, must be moral, must adapt itself to the needs of its members so as to enlarge their measure of life, that the poet is right when he says, "Ill fares the land, to hastening ills a prey, where wealth accumulates while men decay."

Many individuals in the Society of Friends are saying that they must re-examine a system where, in the most prosperous periods, over thirty per cent of the people live on less than one thousand dollars a family, while less than one-third of one per cent of the people receive seventeen per cent of the entire income of the country; and where less than five per cent of the people get over thirty-five per cent of the national income, while thirty-six thousand families receive as much as do twelve million families at the other end of the scale. Such was the condition in the United States even in 1929.

If incomes had been raised to twenty-five hundred dollars a family for the low income groups this might have absorbed the "overproduction" and the resultant congestion of productive equipment and goods. However, today we face an actual decrease in employment and in production in spite of the increase in population, which fact spells increased misery and damage for the children of this generation.

Two independent forces insist that we face this problem today. One is the rising demand from the people that they share more adequately in the benefit from the things which they help produce, that we return once more to recognize, with Adam Smith, that "consumption is the sole end and purpose of all production, and that the interest of the producer ought to be attended to only so far as it may be necessary for promoting that of the consumer." [1]

The other force driving us to this conclusion is the fact that high productivity is our basic need and that this can be maintained only under a high degree of equitable distribution, where "surplus profits" are kept down and where the enjoyment of the goods produced is passed out to those people who share in their production. The ultimate aim of economic society is to make good consumers out of its citizens, providing them with opportunity for the abundant life. Moreover, the immediate

[1] Adam Smith, *The Wealth of Nations*, Harvard Classics edition, Vol. 10, p. 444.

need of the industrial system itself is for a consuming public with greater buying power. Today we begin to see that the welfare of the people makes prosperity—even the prosperity of the corporations themselves. We have been mistaken in thinking that manipulative profits made a real prosperity. Now we see that distributed prosperity makes continued profits possible; it is not exploitation but the steady flow of economic activity that is successful and desirable.

Growing numbers of Friends, in America, as well as in England and Australia, are being pressed on from this point to inquire into the justice and propriety of a so-called "profit system" where growth and concentration of power give to a few absolute control over the destiny of so many lives, including women and children in the homes as well as all those at work. Friends approve pay for productive activity of management, and of owners and their capital, but they do seriously question the equity of putting *control* entirely into the hands of these few.

Moreover many Quakers are re-examining the question of liberty, finding that equality of bargaining power is essential to any real freedom of contract or freedom of enterprise. They see that otherwise this "freedom" may turn out to be a hollow mockery for those men who have only time, skill, energy and the needs of their families to safeguard, or to sell.

It is easy to indicate faults of the present order.

But to choose the proper basis for distributing the income of the nation among the wage-earners, the rent-receivers, the interest-receivers, and the profit-receivers is one of the most baffling problems of our age.

While the problem of rent-taking—the appropriation by private owners of the natural resources —is one of the basic questions for any social order, this may be dismissed here with a word. Friends have not thought through the application of their New Testament principles to this question. Several individuals are attacking it but not the Society generally as yet.

Friends have never strictly held to a bargaining theory which says in essence "that they should take who have the power, and they should keep who can." They have insisted always upon "liberality to the poor" and provision for the unfortunates. They have extolled the excellence of the "middle station in life," where one avoided the dangers of riches on the one hand and the devastating results of poverty on the other. They have endeavored to distribute education widely, ever since the days when George Fox planned for a system of schools and helped to prepare text books. They have pioneered in social work, in prison reform, and in orphanages, in care for the blind and the insane, but they have endeavored to avoid pauperizing their own members or others. Many of them are asking seriously, now, for a sound basis for sharing the good things of life. Should this be on

the basis of productivity, effort, willingness, bargaining power, need, or on some combination of
these? What should be the goal of the nation in
its distributive policy? Should families and their
needs enter into consideration? Should the nation's
need for effective citizens be a factor? Should
other things be used as are schools, libraries, parks
and highways—according to the capacity for making good use of them?

In the past men have been looked upon as objects for exploitation on two sides—on one as
"hands" or workers to be used as much as possible
for as little reward as was necessary, and on the
other as consumers who were to be charged "as
much as the traffic would bear"—without too much
concern for quality and healthfulness. Now we
begin to realize that it is both good fellowship and
good religion, as well as good business, to treat
men as *men*—to learn that industry was made for
man and not man for industry.

The freedom of the market economy, giving
room for the exercise of individual choice and
variation in taste, appeals to Friends. They desire
to preserve our open-class society where the social
elevators go both up and down and where the
doors swing both in and out. But does this require
highly concentrated control and exploitation? Does
this render it impossible to make industry the servant of man instead of his master? Does this mean
that in the struggle for survival the rewards must

go to those best fitted to *"thrive on society"* instead of those best fitted to serve society?

Friends had the answer in early days when industrial relations were personal. They insisted that since there was "that of God" in servants as well as masters these be treated accordingly. But they do not have the complete answer for the new world yet. If there is something of God in every man, if human life is sacred, what about the right to work, or to strike, and what about honest workmanship?

Many are asking these questions as insistently as the early Friends of Germantown asked their disturbing questions about slavery. Already they see that an interest-bearing credit (or debt) economy, operating under the control of those seeking "profits" and "rents" does not give an equitable or functional distribution when competition is so far hindered and removed as in major cases in present-day life. They want to know what would take place if the social order based its activity on that philosophy which prevailed among early Friends.

Every system of distribution is largely an institutional, or governmental, system whether so recognized or not. The frame of government, the ordinary laws of business, and the corporation laws affect this problem mightily. Moreover the tax theory and policy of the government—including the debt policy and money program as well as the tariff schedule—all these vitally affect the lives of the people. Quaker economists today are pointing out that a people get real wealth, not by exhausting their natural resources and shipping the products away, but by receiving want-satisfying goods to enjoy. This suggests that nations in their scramble to get rid of their economic goods are still more short-sighted when they *force* these on other peoples and spend great sums for so-called "national defense" to make secure this denuding of their native land. A more rational plan would seem to be the exchange of those goods and services of which a nation has a comparative abundance for those which are relatively scarce. This would at the same time make it possible for customer nations to continue to purchase those things which they most need. Many Quaker teachers think a policy of trade and money based on this idea of mutual advantage might go far toward removing the strife between nations today.

While co-operation actually is the basic process of our economic order it is submerged, too often, by motives of struggle and combat. In this day of unequal control of resources and market, and of unequal power, it is tragic for men to rely on old motives to provide for human need. Today, as always, the type of social organization and the type of men in charge both affect the chance which the people have at life.

Numerous individuals sense the fact there is going on today a new social and spiritual revolution. One phase of this is the widening conception of property and property-rights. Actually the real thing in property is not the tangible or material thing but the "bundle of rights" to use and control the materials. These "rights" are granted by society and change from time to time. It is expected that the present movement may lead to the extension of property rights to include the right to work, to the use of energy, skill, and time productively. It must be noted here that Friends have never assumed that the present law was final or unchangeable. From the very first they have been willing to suffer peaceably for the sake of bringing legal requirements into line with the higher moral law. Some of them expect that again they may have a share in reshaping the laws and requirements of governments—not through self-seeking or anti-social activity but through a higher social loyalty—through socialized disobedience if necessary.

### THE CONFUSION IN FRIENDS' VIEWS

As indicated above Friends are *aware* of a new inconsistency of life and are coming to realize that this must be faced, but the meaning of all this for the Society and for the individuals has not become clear. Groups of Friends, as well as individuals, are now challenging the injustices and imperfections of the industrial order, as we shall note later; but they have not influenced the Society itself very profoundly as yet.

Those persons who have seen the complacency

and smug respectability within the Society in recent years are now delighted to see the evidence of new life as shown by the uneasy stirrings in so many centers. Great confusion there is, certainly, but this in itself is an evidence that Friends' principles are moving forward into new territory.

One prominent Friend remarked not long ago, "Can't we do away with this urge to service . . . all this panic to reform?" On another occasion just such a Friend said she "expected to cling to her standard of living, that this was needed for her personality development . . . that it was as easy for a rich person to rise above too much as for a poor person to rise above too little."

Another wealthy Friend remarked recently that he was "against all this idea of education for the people, that it put ideas into their heads."

Friends are found, in many parts of America at least, to have absorbed the viewpoints and moral standards of their various communities. So while Quakerism stood, once, as a challenge to the blind customs and *mores,* it often accepts these now, merely giving them a little "Quaker flavor."

However, there are many who realize that "there is a fundamental inconsistency between the present economic and political order and the Sermon on the Mount." They believe this will continue except as changed by our movement toward the Kingdom of God. Therefore their proposal is that we move in that direction as rapidly as possible, asking that steps for change bring not sudden perfection but real improvement.

The differences found between various groups of Friends are illustrated by the fact that when the joint Social Order Committee (including prominent Quaker employers) sent a committee to visit the President of the United States to urge his support of the famous section seven A [2] of the National Recovery Act another group of Friends were telling their Bible-Class teacher that it was inappropriate to discuss this Act or the needs which prompted it, in Friends' gatherings. A spokesman said, "After all, this is a religious group," and that "we ought to seek the *religious* basis in our study instead of criticizing the industrial system."

However, others, in conversation and in their Friends' papers, are asking seriously whether there can be any spiritual revival among Friends until they cut loose from paganism on this new front . . . the economic order.

Here, then, is the stage of life all set for a new moral drama. Friends now fixed in respectable middle-class society in a business-state stage of civilization at the same time have in their midst the inner religious impulse and its ceaseless demand for consistent social action.

[2] This provided for protection to labor and also its right to organize and do collective bargaining.

# The Economic Life

There are two distinct phases of the Quaker approach to practical problems. One is found in the way in which they conduct themselves in existing situations. If these are beyond their control they peacefully submit, but abstain from participating in vicious activity. In early days a Quaker store-keeper turned out to be a better store-keeper, a Quaker brewer a better brewer, a Quaker slave-owner a better slave-owner. This way of life accounts in some measure for the Quaker dominance of the candy and chocolate industries in England today, an explanation of which would have to reach from their plantations in Africa to their planned factory communities with all of their provision for physical and cultural needs of the workers. Three great firms are notable for the degree to which they have modified and broadened the base of their activities within the capitalistic system. Another well-known example is that of Morris E. Leeds' activity in extending control and benefits through a plan of joint management and ownership of the Leeds and Northrup Company, in Philadelphia.

The second part of the Quaker emphasis is found in the way they have always challenged evil systems which are exhibited in the personal treatment of unfortunates or in the working of an economic order which on the one hand manipulates for the gain of the small group and on the other chooses policies regardless of effect on abandoned villages or stranded families, whose workers may have been life-long employees.

Friends never have lacked entirely for leaders in either of the above types of activity. Fox himself strongly emphasized both sides of the attack. Unfortunately, most of his social message is found in the eight volumes of his "works" while too many of those studying Quakerism have contented themselves with the *Journal* alone. His letter "To all Magistrates in London," his "Warning to all Merchants," or his letter to the King of Spain will convince the reader of Fox's readiness to attack the social practices of his day. In his "Men's coming up from the North," Fox said, "O England . . . thou grindest the face of the poor and liftest thyself up in thy pride."

Penn, in his *Commentary upon the Present Condition of the Kingdom,* written in 1677, said, "As all laws and governments design the benefit of the people governed, that there be harmony and agreement with all parts thereof, so everything that causes disagreement must be expelled." Francis Howgill said in his "A Woe to Magistrates": [3]

"You lofty ones of the earth who have gotten much of the creation into your hands and thereby set your nests on high

[3] The above selections are quoted from Fox's Works; see the present writer's manuscript, *Creative Peace-Making in the Society of Friends,* and Philip S. Belasco's *Authority in Church and State.* The last book is a very valuable study of Quakerism in public life.

and are become Lords of your brethren . . . and he who gets the greatest share shall become the greatest man, and all that have little shall bow down and worship him and so break the command of God. . . . The cries of the poor whom you have oppressed and whose labours you have spent upon the lusts—the rust of your gold and silver doth witness."

It is true then that the social message of the Quakers is not a new thing but that it is now experiencing a new awakening. So it is delightful to find present-day Friends "discovering" one of their own early prophets, John Bellers, through Karl Marx who referred to Bellers as a phenomenon in history. This mild Quaker long ago contended that "labor creates wealth instead of wealth providing for labor." He proposed schools and industrial communities, planned for the aid of the common people.

Today Quaker economists, business leaders, and others are confronted by a "competitive" order far different from that dreamed of by earlier writers. The "imperfect competition" between giant organizations is often overshadowed by agreements, by "associations," by "institutes," by "cartels," while the competition is left largely to laborers seeking work with these highly organized employers. Here competition does not always serve the general welfare through providing high quality and low prices. Indeed the "fittest to survive" may at times prove to be those fittest to thrive on society, as said above.

Some Friends, moreover, are uneasy over the appearance of what they consider an "unholy trinity" of imperialistic capitalism, materialistic nationalism, and modern militarism. They see the threat of a new competition between the "Uncle Sams" of the world and fear that this will not always bring the benefits of an "over-ruling Providence." Friends desire real liberty and invigorating individualism for persons and states, but not economic anarchy when it is ruthless or individualism when it becomes selfish greed. They see that we cannot sow the seeds of war in exploitation without reaping that war. Economic war fruits in military war and exploitation bears its harvest in revolution. Friends are coming to understand, also, that in this complex civilization all are involved, personally, in the acts of the nation and of the industrial order. There are no "moral holidays" for the Quaker and no escapes from moral responsibility for the acts of our society. This idea is taking root again as it did in the early life of the Society. In order to survive a democracy must be real in practice as well as in form, its unity must include the political, economic, and spiritual life of the people.

In 1910 English Friends said in their *Discipline:*[4]

"In making an income, whether great or small, the Christian must seek the good of others, and of the community at large, and not simply of himself and his family. He will, even at the risk of loss, strive to be strictly honest and truthful in his dealings; will refuse to manufacture, or deal in articles that are hurtful to society; and will be on his guard against ob-

[4] *Discipline,* London, 1911, p. 95 f.

taining, through monopoly or otherwise, an undue profit at the cost of the community. If he is an investor he will keep these thoughts in mind, and in seeking for investments will think not only of security and the rate of interest, but of the conditions under which his income is produced. . . . Not alone the directors, but also the shareholders of public companies are responsible for the wages paid and the conditions of labour."

The same year Race Street Yearly Meeting said, "Do you recognize your responsibility for just dealing whether as individuals or as members of corporations?"

London Yearly Meeting adopted the well-known statement on "Foundations of a True Social Order" [5] in 1918 in which they urged that

"mutual service should be the principle upon which life is organized. Service, not profit, should be the motive of all work.

"The ownership of material things, such as land and capital should be so regulated as best to minister to the need and development of man."

The "Commission Reports" for the London Conference in 1920 carried the thought much farther. But the next clear step ahead came in 1934 and 1935 in the statements of London Yearly Meeting and of the two Yearly Meetings of Philadelphia. The London Epistle for 1934 stated that: [6]

"there are inequalities of wealth greater than can be justified on any sound principle. . . . The changes . . . necessary . . . include the extension of public ownership or control . . . aiming at the right relationship between private and public interest. In a rightly ordered community, wealth would be held in relation to need, to service, and to the fullness of life for all; and unemployment, as we know it, would not exist.

[5] *Discipline,* London, 1921, p. 121.
[6] *Minutes,* London, 1934, minute 40.

Bertram Pickard, contributing to an extended discussion, said at that time regarding this issue and pacifism:[7]

"Moreover, the Quaker religious intuition is today enormously reinforced by pragmatic considerations. On the one hand, a technical revolution, giving power of unlimited production . . . is in process, I believe, of creating a radical change in the mind of the capitalist. Ruin (and social revolution) stares the modern industrialist in the face unless he will actively cooperate with the national and international community in organizing a planned economy, and in particular the distribution of purchasing power. . . . On the other hand, the disasters that have overtaken proletarian organizations that have played with the idea of armed force, as in Germany and Austria, are a tragic warning to those who consciously or unconsciously cherish the belief that, under modern conditions, the *status quo* might be changed for the good by revolutionary violence."

The Five Years Meeting, representing twelve American Yearly Meetings, made history for that body of Friends, in 1935, when it considered frankly the problems of the economic order in connection with the penetrating report of its Commission dealing with that subject.

Back in 1918 the printed "Extracts" from the reports of a conference of employers, chiefly members of London Yearly Meeting, contained the following headings: Wages, Security of Employment, Working Conditions, Appropriation of "Surplus Profits." These deliberations showed a fearless determination to apply the principles of Jesus to these questions. Since that time the group has been active in re-examining the question of Quakerism

[7] Bertram Pickard, "Quaker Pacifism and Politics," *The Friend*, London, 3:29:1934, p. 317.

in industry, the changes necessary, and the peaceful methods by which they may be secured.

In America the two Philadelphia Yearly Meetings have been feeling their way toward "a righteous social order" for several years, as stated above. The *Discipline* of Arch Street Yearly Meeting, in 1926, affirmed that the "profit motive" was apposed to the teachings of the Sermon on the Mount, while in 1928 the *Discipline* of the General Conference group called on all members to apply in their relations to corporations, in whatever capacity, the same high standards as always applied by Friends in individual business.

This issue was carried farther in 1935 when the report of the Joint Social Order Committee, sent to both Yearly Meetings, indicated that Friends should remove from their thinking "two stumbling blocks": the terms "Socialism" and "the profit motive." They proceeded to contrast "old-style capitalism" and socialism and then considered the possibilities of a "modified capitalism."

The concluding statement indicated that the social order was of tremendous importance to the "physical well-being and the spiritual quality of our life," that it was capable of human direction, that the present situation presaged civil and foreign strife and war, that our "progress" was largely mechanical and at the expense of the spirit of man. The following statement closed the report and is given here since it indicates the economic views of many of the leaders and teachers among Friends today: [8]

"We affirm our belief that the principal and most vital change required in the social order is one whereby the proceeds of the labor of individuals can in much larger measure be returned to the individuals who perform the labor; whereby the investment and administration of capital shall be guided by the social usefulness of the proposed product of the investment, and the expectation of a reasonable and moderate return; and whereby the great spread between the incomes of the rich and of the poor shall be steadily diminished until there shall no more exist the very great fortunes and the extreme poverty now characteristic of American life.

"We affirm our belief that the principle of social control, or ownership and control, should be gradually extended, as may be practicable, so as to cover an increasing area in the general field of industry, including at least public utilities and public transportation, banking and credit, and mining, lumbering, and other industries closely dependent upon natural resources.

"We affirm further our belief that wherever the world's work is done, the incentives arising from the various rewards of society to the individual can and should be made to stimulate the life of the spirit rather than the desire for money and power. We believe it is possible, and we would do our part, to create a social order in which, as a matter of course, men will receive recompense according to their needs in return for the best service they can render, and in which the emphasis is not upon material gain, but upon sweetness, simplicity, and spiritual depth as exemplified in the life of the Master."

The reader should be reminded that the above is not a "representative view." No doubt the majority of Friends would not endorse it even today. But the present writer has found that the trend of thought in the Society is not indicated by a cross section or "balance sheet" so much as by the trend of thought among those sensitive leaders who

[8] *The Friend,* Supplement, Philadelphia, 3:14:1935.

steadily point out inconsistencies in behavior and among their followers who carry the problem to other groups.

One John Woolman outweighed a hundred slave-owners, as did one Fox a regiment. It appears now that a few open-minded and spiritually guided employers may outweigh a thousand who unthinkingly accept the social and moral views of their communities.

### FRIENDS SEEK THE CREATIVE WAY IN INDUSTRY

Quakerism, like early Christianity, has not been given to endorsement either of specific forms of government or of industrial society. Its great emphasis has been laid upon peacable and constructive ways of behavior, within whatever frame of government or business might be prevalent. As we have seen, Friends have been characterized by a workable blend of group-mysticism and group-determined social behavior, where a fine balance between the individual and the social aspects of life was preserved.

Wherever Quakerism manifested its essence, in home, school, trade, or public affairs it played a creative, experimental role. In numberless cases this *way* is being tried out today by the Friends Service Council and the American Friends Service Committee as well as by business firms. Indeed Friends probably are as well known for their creative peace-making behavior as for their "religious" beliefs.

While these Friends do not yet have a complete answer as to *how* to make industry spiritually creative they are making headway in this arena, just as they did in slowly moving into the arenas of drunkenness, war, and slavery. In each case it was a tentative, groping pacifism that had to grow into virility.[9]

This brings us to the heart of the Quaker message on the economic problem. It appears to be true that the real opportunity for Friends today lies in working out effective peace-making methods for industry. While many differ on various points they all can unite in seeking to make the peace-maker's spirit and technique effective in this new area of life. Forms of society are always shifting but principles of action must be creative for the real Quaker. He must seek that creative way of living which meets and removes conflict. Today as always Quakerism appeals to those in seats of oppression, offering to them a better way; and at the same time it offers to the oppressed and disinherited a religiously warmed love and fellowship. There is still that energizing core of ideals, or religious values, which works away to revive the spiritual life and the practical message.

[9] In Indiana, for example, when a few young Friends denounced slavery as an economic order they were disowned. But a little later the Society had abandoned its old position and its hesitancy for a vigorous clear-cut position which led even to disowning those who had not rid themselves of that economic system.

Recently one of the leaders, most devoted to reliance on spiritual methods alone, said in the presence of the writer:

"How can we live with a free conscience in an outrageously unjust world? . . . The revolution of brotherly love is possible only as we adopt the Christ spirit as our own. Christ requires that we adopt true objectives."

Today Quakerism rises again to challenge that life based on exploitation, where men are "used as tools" and again exploited as consumers. It teaches that economic society is essentially co-operative in nature and that legitimate trade is of mutual benefit, whether between persons or nations. It teaches that the ultimate survival of any system or civilization must be left to its effect on the human beings concerned. Moreover, it teaches that the way to prove the supremacy of the spiritual is, not by ignoring its practical implications, but by demonstrating the power of the spiritual in transforming the economic and social life of the people.

Quakers believe that time is on the side of God and His purposes, and that God dares trust the ways of democracy rather than the way of tyranny and dictatorship. Otherwise He would never have tolerated the age-long folly of man, they say. Friends do not line up and take sides. They take principles of action and let the sides take the consequences. They accept neither type of radicalism popular today. Reactionary radicalism would seize control and freeze the social order in a position where it would protect vested interests regardless of the wider human cost involved. Revolutionary radicalism would abandon ideals and spirit for violent destruction of the old order in the belief that a better order would thus be established.

Quakers do not endorse violence and destruction either in the name of reaction and oppression or in the name of resentment and revolution. They seek to change, peacefully, the controls of the social order so as to make for genuine freedom and for the release of creative life. They appeal now to both parties in the industrial struggle to try creative ways. They say to conservatives, "The only way to conserve your system is to humanize it and actually to use the spirit of democracy," and they say to labor and to the disinherited, "The only way to win in your struggle for a chance at life is to make effective the methods of non-violence and to demonstrate the virile strength of organized, determined love."

Friends are not afraid of revolutionary changes, so long as these move toward constructive ends and apply creative methods. In this sense the New Testament is a book of revolution precisely because it is a book of revelation. For Quakerism holds that the greatest constructive revolution in history is the change wrought in society through the peaceful application of the ideals and purposes, the spirit and teaching, the life and methods of Jesus. One cause for rejoicing is that in this sense there *are* "more worlds to conquer."

# IX

## THE INDIVIDUAL AND THE STATE

*Walter C. Woodward, Ph.D.*
Editor of the American Friend

HOW does the Quaker's strong commitment to democracy inhere in the central principle of his religious faith? And if committed to democracy, how can he justify an appeal to conscience as above the law of the democratic State?

> "Your Gaoles we fear not,
>     no, nor banishment.
> Terrors nor threats can ere make
>     us lament.
> For such we are as fear the liveing God,
> Not being vexed by persecution's Rod.
> Away hippocrisie, adew false fear,
> Immortal life's the crown which we doe bear,
> Which cannot be removed from us away.
> That makes us scorn your
>     threatenings every day.
> These are our prayers & thus
>     our Souls doe cry—
> Let justice live and all
>     oppression die."
> *—From a collection of early
> Quaker manuscripts.*

Perhaps no subject involves more deeply today the cause of the human good that that of the nature and authority of the State. Whether the issue is thrust brusquely and even brutally upon us by ruthless dictatorship, or whether through gradual extension of function by peaceful penetration, the question presents itself to us all as one of those irrespressible conflicts which commands our anxious attention. It is the purpose of the writer to present as comprehensively as may be the Christian approach to the conception of the State, and the relation of the individual to the latter in the light of Quaker thought and practice.

Briefly, first, may we review the rise of the modern theory of the State, grounded in the doctrine of absolute sovereignty. In the break-up of the Roman Empire, Europe fell apart into many, many fragments, whose relations with each other were quite generally those which prevail between rival bandits, and whose internal conditions were but too anarchic. While the gradual development of feudal relationships gave a semblance of order, Europe went into long eclipse, politically, in an age of chaotic confusion.

With the period of exploration and discovery, the extension of trade and commerce, and the development of city life, this anarchic situation became increasingly intolerable. There was a demand for such order and stability of government as would give security and opportunity of progress. Centrifugal forces of society had too long run riot in their destructiveness. The need was for centralization and authority, for a State with power to curb factious individualism. Out of the welter of anarchy and contending forces, out of the strife among feudal powers, there gradually arose above their competitors, by sheer force and fortune, certain princes and houses which developed the necessary strength and prestige as the basis of the nascent modern State. The required centralized authority which the troublous times demanded, these powerful princes developed. The growing conception was a natural one which identified them and the power they exerted with the State, the framework for which they constructed.

Here, as usual, political philosophy or theory followed the facts to justify and explain them. With the divisive civil and religious strife in France as the background of his thought, the French writer Bodin presented the first definite, systematic conception of the sovereignty of the State—of a State which, through its ruler, could justly require the unquestioning obedience of all. The foundation was thus laid in *theory* for the *fact* of the supremacy of the State.

On the foundation laid by Bodin, other political theorists builded. Notably Hobbes, who, in the following century, so developed the theory of sovereignty as to justify absolutism. That his purpose was to uphold the despotism of the Stuarts does not shake his hard logic nor weaken his bold conception of the absolute power of the State, a power so inescapable, so terrible, as to justify his naming it after the monster, Leviathan. This marked the high tide of the theory as applied to the support of autocracy.

With the countercurrent of constitutionalism,

and later of democracy, the conception of the power of the State was largely maintained, though the exercise of that power was given a democratic instead of an autocratic basis. Going from one extreme to the other, Rousseau so constructed the State, theoretically, as to locate its sanction in the will of the people. As a matter of fact, the impersonal and absolute nature of his collective or mob rule predicated a Leviathan no less ominous than that of Hobbes.

While still enamored of the doctrine of political sovereignty, some later thinkers sought to soften and liberalize this absolute conception of the State. Though the final and supreme authority of the latter was assumed, the State was made to be beneficent in purpose and function, emphasizing the personal welfare and development of its citizens. Rarely, except in time of national emergency, was it necessary for the State to invoke to the full its sovereign power, imposing its will upon all dissentients, and even suspending, as in time of war, its orderly and constitutional process. Thus it was that democratic ideals were seen to prosper. The inalienable rights of the individual were apparently safeguarded rather than jeopardized by a State that was benevolently authoritative, with the result that the inherent issue between individual liberty and State authority was seldom joined.

Today, however, the world has been rudely awakened from the fancied security of democratic ideals. A new theory of the State is arrogantly propounded, more menacing to the people as persons than any doctrine of autocracy and absolutism ever embodied in governmental forms. Again, the theory has been developed to explain and justify the *fait accompli;* which it does in a manner as thoroughgoing and contemptuous of personal values as the practice has been ruthless. For the new State is not only omnipotent—it is entirely what its name signifies—totalitarian. The State becomes not an instrument but an end—a sacred entity, to be deified. It is not created to serve the purpose of men as personalities, but to submerge and absorb them. There are no individual rights to be recognized, much less observed. Democratic ideals and processes are not merely ignored—they are brazenly decried. This new monster Leviathan dominates every phase of human life, it enters every sphere of individual conduct. No chamber of the heart, no cloister of the soul is inviolate to its intrusion. Personality, the purpose and goal of creation, ceases to exist. Never has the Christian ideal of life been negated so absolutely—never have liberal ideals of human devolopment been flouted more thoroughly.

This imperious challenge would be serious enough could the regime it represents be confined to those countries in which it holds undisputed sway. But ideas cannot be isolated. Strange as it may seem, the doctrine of totalitarianism has its eager devotees in lands of the democratic tradition, and while they may never succeed in changing the form of government therein, there is scarcely less threat to democratic principles in the increasing assertion of those forces in the body politic that are too nearly one in spirit with the totalitarian practice.

Squarely, therefore, and inescapably is the issue of freedom and personality versus State absolutism and compulsion thrust upon us. The situation, thus boldly limned in today's political sky, but serves to accentuate the problem which the discerning Christian has always faced, at least partially, and the Quaker actually, in seeking to establish a right relationship with the State, to which they acknowledge allegiance and desire to yield obedience.

It has been said that Friends have never worked out fully a philosophy of the State. This is true. However, such a philosophy is more or less implicit in their very definite conception of human personality. This conception is at the very heart of their faith. God breathed something of His spirit into man and he became a sacred person, a temple of the Divine on earth. Personality, with all its potentialities, is the supreme value in the world. It is the channel and expression of God's purpose for His kingdom among men. There is no meaning or significance to life and world events apart from human personality. It is the pulsating, sentient force, the very soul of what we call society.

What are some of the implications which derive from this central principle of Friends as they relate to the State? Since persons are paramount, those governmental arrangements are best which give the freest and fullest play to individual development. To such development an atmosphere of friendliness and co-operation is essential. Compulsion may successfully regiment people in the mass but it is deadly to people as persons. All the individual freedom compatible with wholesome social relationships is requisite to true progress. While such freedom is possible under varying forms of government, it bespeaks the essence of democracy in spirit and practice. Just as the central core of the Quaker faith implies a spiritual democracy of believers, so does this faith carry over into a political democracy of doers. Indeed we may well question the expression "carry over," inasmuch as the Friend views life as a unit, rather than as divided into two compartments, spiritual and secular. Under this conception, wherein all life is considered a sacrament, government, or the State, is not looked upon as secular and apart but is brought within the circle of Friendly concern.

The Quaker experience of personality is primarily mystical; the individual soul and God are in immediate communion. But this is not a mysticism of retreat or isolation. Because the Friend has the sense of the divine inflowing, he realizes that this is an experience universally possible. Every human heart, potentially at least, is a temple of God, and is therefore sacred. The Friend becomes solicitous, accordingly, for the welfare of all men everywhere, his spiritual brothers; solicitous for their physical as well as their spiritual well-being, believing that nothing that affects personality is foreign to the divine concern.

Now the State, through its governmental functions, has the power of life and death over its citizens. When enlightened and benevolent in purpose, it can do much to futher the welfare of its people. It may become an agency for advancing Christ's kingdom on earth through the means at its command for helping lift men from conditions which hinder their true growth and development. Early Friends were quick to appreciate the possibility. Even while they themselves were suffering for their convictions at the hand of the State, their social concern drew them to a crusade for human welfare in which they sought the aid which the arm of the government was able, if disposed, to give. Quite early in his career, for example, we find George Fox appealing to Parliament to provide work for the unemployed as a means not only of reducing the ranks of the so-called criminal class, but of making men self-respecting through honest labor.

As further basis of Friendly interest in the State, we turn again to the Quaker emphasis upon personality. Its inspiration and dynamic are inward; its flowering in service is outward. Personalities develop, not separately in seclusion, but together. This is illustrated in the Quaker meeting for worship. Friends as individuals "center down" into quiet waiting and meditation, each seeking to worship in spirit and in truth. These seeking Friends are often fused into oneness of spirit, out of which there is a corporate leading or expression which is much more than the sum of the individual experiences. The experience is not confined to spiritual services, so-called. Inasmuch as to the Quaker all life is a sacrament, all our daily associations may be similarly creative, through the interplay of personalities in mutual influence. Hence the importance of keeping free, invigorating and wholesome the conditions under which personalities develop and achieve progress through such interplay. While by no means the only association or institution through which persons become effective in society, the importance of the State in this respect is obvious. And all these and other requisites for the fullest development of personality and the right ordering of human relationships imply a liberal, democratic State: the kind of State envisaged in the following paragraph, quoted from the Anglo-Irish Commission Report made in connection with the Friends' World Conference in 1937:

"Our conception of the State, or of the nation as politically organized, is that it is in essence and intention a piece of combined action for the good of each and all: and it should take the shape of a free and friendly commonwealth. We have seen the close relation of our faith to that of democracy. Government must be, in as real a sense as possible, *by* as well as *for* the people. The greatest number possible must be given the opportunity for, and stimulated to develop, an active concern for the common weal. Deprive them of this and you limit their manhood and cut at the root of progress. We believe that there cannot be any barrier or rigid frontier between the sphere of religion and what are thought of as the secular interests of life. We hold that everyone, and not a few specialists only, still less some self-appointed 'supermen,' is to be accounted a channel through which light and guidance may come. It follows that we need to create the widest opportunity for the free play of thought and the free sharing of counsel upon questions of common concern."

It might be assumed that Friends, so eager to realize a State of this beneficent nature, would participate actively in official, governmental life to help bring it to pass. Several factors have operated to preclude general participation in politics. Historically, Friends were first a proscribed group in England. They were the objects rather than the subjects of government! Their initial opposition to an established, authoritative Church brought them under the penalties of the State which sought to enforce conformity. They were definitely without the pale. Later, Friends tended to lapse for a time from their eager social concern into a period of quietism, and admonished each other to "keep quiet in the land." From a prominent Quaker preacher, Thomas Shillitoe, came this deliverance: "Friends, let us not dare to meddle with political matters but renewedly seek for holy help to starve that disposition. Keep that ear closed which will be itching to hear the news of the day. Avoid reading political publications and as much as possible, newspapers." This attitude, however, represented a flight from the "full gospel" of the

Quaker faith and was far from expressive of true Friendly concern.

When religious toleration was approximated, Friends were still practically eliminated from political life because of their refusal to take the oath of office. Joseph Pease entered the first reformed Parliament in 1833 on affirmation, the first Quaker actually to take his seat in that body. Soon after, John Bright, exemplar of the Christian in public life, began his great Parliamentary career. In later times, English Friends in considerable number have participated in government in Parliament, in municipal offices and in judicial posts.

In America, the sequence, singularly enough, has been somewhat reversed. In the earlier period, Friends were quite prominently identified with public affairs, while in later years their public service has not been significant. Despite the various inhibitions against dissenters in general, and Quakers and Catholics in particular, by force of character and leadership they held public office in several of the Colonies—were often in legislative assemblies, and in judicial and executive positions. In a few notable instances, the Quakers dominated public life for an extended period. Note, for example, a Quaker governor of Rhode Island leading the Colonial Assembly to mid-week Quaker Meeting!

Unfortunately, however, while Quaker governors could lead their assemblies and constituents to meeting, they could not always make them drink

at the fount of Quaker principles. And thereby
arose perplexing problems for which there has
never been conclusive answer. Even in Pennsylvania, the scene of William Penn's "Holy Experiment" in government, the Quakers in power found
themselves, in a sense, misrepresenting a non-
Quaker constituency. In the scheme of free, representative government, how far should a public official yield his own convictions in favor of the convictions of those whom he represents? As popularly conceived, force and military defense form
the basis of State authority. What course is open
and justifiable for a responsible Quaker executive
—or legislator—to follow in the premises? To
what extent are accommodation and compromise
justified on the plea that it is better to yield and
accomplish a part of one's high civic purpose than
to stand firm and get nothing? Is it perhaps wiser
not to become compromised in actual participation
in public life, but to bring the full impact of one's
influence upon governmental policy from the outside? These are perplexing and perennial questions
which Friends—and other Christians—face and
answer variously. In general there is perhaps much
greater unity in the principles we hold as related
to the State than in the practice of getting them
incorporated into State action.

We have shown how democracy is inherent in
the Quaker conception of religion and life. Yet we
find that Friends on occasion have resolutely opposed themselves to acts of democratic government,

# The Individual and the State

even to the extent of withholding obedience to them. Is there a paradox here in the Quaker attitude? If democracy is right as the fullest expression of a free people, is not obedience to its mandates, as given in the voice of the majority, obligatory upon us? What becomes of democratic institutions if citizens, having espoused the principles of free government, consider themselves justified in declining to obey laws that are repugnant to them?

To these and similar queries Friends have made rather consistent reply throughout their history—a reply which has more often been embodied in courageous action than in formal declaration. In the first place there is raised the question of primary allegiance. It may be truly said that all Christians face the question as to whether, when loyalties come into conflict, they shall obey God rather than man, or the State. But to the mystically minded Friend, the very presumption of ultimate, external authority "strikes at my life," as George Fox would say. That life in its spiritual essence flows directly from God Himself, who speaks to man through the Inward Light, through the Christ within, and through continuous communion. When an issue of obedience to authority is raised, for the Friend it is not a choice to be made between one external authority, the State, and another external authority, the Church, or even the Book. His choice is between an outer, a human authority, and an inner and spiritual one. Given the Divine Light, as it illuminates life in general, and the question at issue in particular, he must give obedience to it above all else. To yield that is to yield all that makes life meaningful. Whether the opposing claim for obedience is made by a totalitarian or democratic State is irrelevant.

In the second place, the deepest significance of democracy is not in majority domination, but in the opportunity afforded of achieving progress through the democratic process of give and take, of reasonableness, of conference, of mutual co-operation. As Arthur E. Morgan has aptly put it, "Democracy is a spirit of social behavior, not a particular device of government." We must urge the fact again, of the primacy of personality. Democracy is justified and exalted, not by the perfection of political machinery which declares and sanctions a majority vote, but by providing and safeguarding the fullest measure of freedom for the development of persons in their various relationships.

By the manner in which they conduct their own meetings for business, Friends indicate their belief that democracy is a method as well as a principle. Action is had, not by stating a question and putting it to vote, whereby the will of a small majority may be imposed upon a very substantial minority. Without the formality of a motion, the question, concisely presented, is fully considered in an effort to arrive at a common understanding. If there is quite general agreement, the "sense of the meeting" is so declared by the clerk. If there is any considerable dissent, the question is held open for further consideration, or else a modified agreement is reached that the meeting as a whole approves. This expresses the Friendly conception of democracy in process, whereby every due respect is given personal conviction. Progress by accommodation is more slow—and more sure. It is true, obviously, that this simple procedure of a small, homogeneous group, cannot be followed by a large State of complex organization. It does, however, suggest the spirit which should permeate the State in the deference it should have for its citizens as persons, and for the concern it should manifest for giving due weight to minority opinion.

In taking their stand for the exercise of a free conscience in a democratic State, Friends feel deeply that instead of being subversive of the State, they are rendering it the very highest service. Holding to a single standard of morality for the individual and for the political group, they believe that the State should be and can be Christianized. But how can this be done except free expression of Christian conviction be honored? Certainly not by suppressing and penalizing consciences courageous enough to brave the consequences of disobedience in order to be true to the heavenly vision. To the objection that conceding the right of conscientious objection would open the way to abuses of private privilege of dissent, it is pointed out that there is a great difference between the wanton assumption of disregard of law for personal desire and selfish interest, and the deeply considered conviction of the Christian who cannot violate the sacred shrine which God has established within him. As the Five Years Meeting Commission stated in 1935, "The risks of granting the autonomy of conscience in a loyal citizenship are small compared to the inevitable danger of a people without an active and dominant conscience. Since the Quaker's conscience is motivated by the Fatherly love of God and directed by Jesus' ideal of brotherly love, it could be a menace only to a State whose policies contemplated injustice to a class, race or other nation. Such a policy must, if our faith in Christ be true, do more damage to a people, than could the possible vagaries of a few perverted consciences."

The Quaker position on this whole question was well summed up in the following words written by T. Edmund Harvey in the London *Friend* in 1914:

"It has been urged that while we owe much to the religious community to which we belong, we owe a greater allegiance to the wider community of the State. This is a position which the early Christians had constantly to face. Their answer led to martyrdom, but were they wrong? Beyond the State we love and honor, we must look up to that eternal Commonwealth whose citizens we are called to be. . . . What is the duty of the individual citizen in a State only imperfectly Christian, with still much of Pagan in it? To the Christian, loyalty to the spirit of Christ must come before obedience to the State, and it will only be by the increasing faithfulness of a growing number of individuals to the Christian ideal that the State itself will have its standards raised."

## The Individual and the State

Although the Quaker position on war is not the immediate concern of this chapter, brief reference to it is pertinent for the reason that it is just here that the Friendly will comes into most frequent conflict with the will of the State; and for more than one reason. First, because war, with all its accompaniments, is the very antithesis of the Quaker interpretation of the religion of Jesus; and second, because its spirit and method are the negation of those orderly, reasonable, democratic processes that are most wholesome and constructive.

The peace position of the Society of Friends is central to its fundamental principle. It is inwardly inspired, not outwardly enjoined. Even if there were no church pronouncements and no Biblical injunction against the mass murder which we call war, Friends would be just as strongly committed against it. War does infinitely worse than kill people—it desecrates and destroys their inner being—the temple of the holy within them. It is high crime against man and mortal sin against God, and Friends generally can have none of it. Hence the inevitable conflict in time of war, when the State calls upon its citizens for military service. In declining to respond to that call—and in taking the consequences which are often not light—they believe they are rendering the country they love a much nobler service by bravely maintaining the testimony of the better way.

Critics of this position are prone to confuse the issue by calling Friends inconsistent in their attitude toward the use of force. "You accept police protection," they say, "and yet you repudiate the work of the army which represents the police of the State in protecting the nation against its enemies." There are several things to be urged in reply to this false analogy. Suffice it here to say that Friends do not absolutely repudiate all force as such, although they minimize its function in government. They do distinguish between a domestic force, under civilian auspices and subject to judicial safeguards, and the kind of unrestrained force exercised by an army, not upon an individual culprit for the purpose of bringing him to court, but indiscriminately upon men, women and children for the purpose of imposing submission through wholesale destruction. Two entirely different things are involved, both in method and principle.

Quite manifest are the implications of life and conduct which derive from the Quaker's appeal from the authority of the State to the higher law of conscience. In the first place, as Elbert Russell has tersely said, "The price of a free conscience must be prepaid." And not only that, but "there is a high maintenance cost." It must be prepaid by a quality of life that leaves no room for question as to the sincerity of his position. Like George Fox, he should be able to say by his daily conduct that he lives in the virtue of that life and power that takes away the occasion of all war—and coercion; that he has come into the "covenant of peace." He should embody among his fellows the spirit of the Christian democracy he espouses: being consistently helpful and conciliatory; generous to the opinions of others—constantly watchful against the inclination to coerce men's minds. There must have been demonstrated in time of peace that positive service of Christian citizenship and constructive loyalty which the Quaker urges when he refuses to do military service in time of war.

And when it comes to a consideration of the "high maintenance cost," some searching questions face the Quaker. Is he willing to give freely of his time and substance in support of the peace movement—willing to sacrifice as much for peace as others do for war? Does he show himself as eager to help forestall war as he is resolute in holding aloof when it comes? How ready is he to forego the advantages which accrue from a nationalist-militarist-economic system which he declines to obey when it calls him to war? Is he as quick to testify against the employment of the armed forces to maintain property rights at home as he is against its use to protect national interests abroad? When it comes to the question of markets, preferential tariffs and immigration, does he take the larger view of the universal human welfare, even to his own seeming hurt? One has but to ask these and similar questions to realize something of the seriousness of the obligation which Friends and others take upon themselves in proclaiming the higher loyalty.

Specifically, in various practical ways Friends have demonstrated the positive, constructive service which may be rendered toward building the kind of Christian State which they envisage. By way of example and suggestion, a few of them are briefly mentioned:

(1) Friends have been active in the leadership of the peace movement, in their respective countries and internationally. Individually, they had much to do with launching the series of international congresses around the middle of the nineteenth century, which eventuated in setting up the Hague Tribunal of arbitration between the nations. The Society of Friends has often constituted the spear-head of the cause of peace, through loyalty to its deep conviction that war is the monster sin against God and man; and perhaps its greatest contribution in this sphere has been the producing of inspired men and women who have been in the van of the march toward peace. An American statesman said, for example, that had there been ten Joseph Allen Bakers in Europe, there would probably have been no World War.

(2) In keeping with their adherence to the democratic method of developing public opinion through information and discussion, Friends have been active in educating the public on the problems of peace and democracy. And because of their belief in universal brotherhood, they have sought to further mutual understanding between people of different countries. In line with this concern,

witness the establishment within recent years of the summer Institutes on International Relations, which have been initiated and developed by Friends in this country till they now extend from coast to coast.

(3) As a small group with an alert social concern, Friends have conducted experiments in human welfare which have pointed the way to State action. Their enlightened attitude toward the insane was the precursor of the modern State hospitals for the mentally sick. Similarly, their concern for the welfare of those in prison is represented by progressive ideals in the State administration of correctional institutions. In this country, particularly in the Middle West, the model of much of our public school system was found in the schools and academies maintained by Friends. In more recent years, Friends in the British Isles and in America have initiated and developed land allotment and subsistence homestead projects which have been suggestive to government of practical projects in the necessary work of rehabilitating those who are the victims of industrial dislocation. Such examples are indicative of the service which may be rendered by a socially adventurous group unreservedly committed to human betterment.

(4) During and following periods of war, Friends have demonstrated their philosophy of peace by enterprises which not only relieved physical need, but testified to the reality of good will: such, for example, as rebuilding demolished

villages in France, feeding the children of an "enemy country," Germany, and now, organizing non-partisan relief for the refugee and orphan children in war-stricken Spain. Such demonstration has been given in connection with industrial-domestic as well as in international warfare. Impartial relief has been given in communities suffering from strike situations; and now the summer volunteer Work Camps are being developed, wherein groups of young people, by daily manual labor, by observation and study, and by free discussion, come to a more sympathetic understanding of conflict situations. Moreover, a positive contribution of service on a definite project is made to the community.

(5) Many Friends, along with others, are gradually waking to the significance of the co-operative movement as embodying the purposes and possibilities of the Chistian democracy for which they stand. They see that political democracy cannot be approximated without substantial economic democracy, and believe it is increasingly doubtful whether the latter can be realized in the present economic set-up. On the one hand Christians exalt the Christlike virtues of love, peace, good will, mutual aid and sacrifice, while on the other hand they maintain stubborn allegiance to the principle of competition which subverts the very virtues they proclaim, in the strife and tension it engenders. Co-operation is seen to be inclusive rather than exclusive, creative rather than destructive of the finest

human values. It is democracy at the source, in practice. Moreover, the co-operative movement, extending across national boundaries, gives a sound basis for international peace. As, through local co-operatives, Friends and fellow Christians establish little enclaves of democracy in a world of competitive strife, they feel that they are building for that co-operative commonwealth which the seers have long visioned as the ideal Christian State.

It is freely said today that democracy faces its major test, beleaguered as it is by the assertive forces of dictatorship. Even in the house of its friends, some counsel that its weaknesses be corrected by the exercise of quasi-dictatorial powers. This is the counsel of defeat. The cure for democracy is more democracy, not less—the democracy of a free, conscientious citizenship. Friends are committed to this increasing Christian purpose, and therefore feel that they are serving the State well by maintaining the rights of conscience in the face of State demands which they cannot obey. However, conscientious objection, important as it may be on occasion, by no means signifies the normal relationship of Friends to their government. Their normal expression is one of conscientious affirmation, in word and deed, of those positive forces of freedom and civic righteousness that truly exalt a nation and make its people to prosper.

# X

## THE CONTROL AND USE OF NATURAL RESOURCES

*J. Russell Smith, Ph.D.*

Professor of Economic Geography, Columbia University

IF the American Indian had destroyed soil and other natural resources in North America as rapidly for 4900 years as the white man has done during the last 100 years, what natural resources would the continent now contain? [1]

In the United States, a land of most abundant resources, millions of people are out of work, want work, and cannot find work, despite the unused resources in every state. Millions are undernourished, ill clothed, and ill housed, experiencing loss of ambition, loss of hope, loss of morals, breakup of family, and personal heartbreak. At the same time our own government and other governments, urged on by pressure groups, pay people to check production and even to destroy crops after they are produced.

Can a Christian or a member of a society that claims friendship or brotherhood among all men approve of such a system, or participate in it without striving to change it?

[1] The answer to this question seems plain: most of it would be essentially a desert. For proof, see reports of U. S. Soil Conservation Service, U. S. Department of Agriculture, Washington, D. C.; reports of the National Resources Board, Washington, D. C.; and *Conservation of Natural Resources in the United States,* Van Hise, C. R., Macmillan, New York.

# The Control and Use of Natural Resources

## I. HISTORICAL DEVELOPMENT OF CONTROL OF RESOURCES

Those who are content with things as they are in the United States are prone to meet the suggestion of economic change by referring to the well known facts that this country is the richest in the world, has developed faster than any other, has for many of its people the best standard of living in the world, and therefore all its systems are good because the good results must be the results of the systems (or form of government, or constitution, or Supreme Court, or "rugged individualism," or whatever it is they are defending). This reasoning is correct only in very small degree. As a matter of fact it is the forces of climate and geology that have showered into the lap of North America abundant natural resources. It is these gifts of nature that have made the United States and Canada far and away the richest countries in the world. During the frontier period, which has now ended, nature almost forced riches upon these peoples.

Another defense of the satisfied mind (or is it pocket book) is to say that we have always had this system, therefore it is good. This also is not true, as a brief examination of origins will show. The almost world-wide practice of primitive man, as well as of the peoples in medieval Europe, seems to show fairly clearly that through most of the tens of thousands of years of the history of the human race most of our ancestors were essentially communists, so far as natural resources were concerned. The wandering tribe had certain pastures *as a tribe*. The village group, when agriculture had begun, had certain lands *as village property,* and the privilege of tilling certain parts was rotated from man to man, from year to year. Parts of this right still persist in the common pastures that belong to the inhabitants of certain Swiss and other European villages.

The disappearance of communal ownership of these village lands is recent, as evidenced by the scores of so-called Enclosure Acts by which the British Parliament (largely 1550-1846) lopped off specific tracts of these semi-public lands and gave them as private property to the friends of the government.

This new monopoly in land was followed in the eighteenth century by a rather extreme development of special trade privileges for special groups, supported by special laws and the regulations of private organizations. This manifested itself in the enactment of tariffs, in the granting of monopolies in the trade of certain articles to individuals, groups, or trade associations such as the guilds. The guilds were organizations made to promote the special advantages of the members, who usually had a monopoly of some branch of production or trade. As described in one of these monopolistic trades they were like certain trade unions in recent times; they usually restricted membership to increase the richness of these monopolies to its members.

Adam Smith's book, *The Wealth of Nations,* published in 1776, was really a protest[2] against this great system of restrictions commonly called Mercantilism. Said he in essence: Throw off restrictions. Let men be free. Abolish the economic lords created by these special favors. Create an economic democracy. Let everyone be free to make a profit. Let men compete for natural resources. Let employers compete for labor. Let laborers compete for jobs. Let everyone be free to take care of himself. That will make the richest and strongest nation.

## The Filling of the Continent

For a century and a quarter (1789-1914) the people of America, acting under the theory of Adam Smith, which happened greatly to please the business interests, were, generation after generation, turned loose in America, the richest of continents. Men had a chance at resources such as they had never had before nor will have again. After the coming of the steamboat, the railroad, and the telegraph, the people settled the country, built farms, towns, communities, states, with a speed unrivaled in human history. The theory was that it was good for man to own land. If he owns land, he will be free; he will be independent; he will

[2] Eli Ginsberg, *The House of Adam Smith.*

care for his own. For generations there was a great effort to get people on the land. Land was almost given away to settlers. In William Penn's day they bought from him for a small price, tracts of land ranging from 70 to 100 acres. In the forests of Pennsylvania such a tract looked large to the man who with ax and horse or ox faced the task of felling the forest and making a farm. After the invention of the reaper, after the discovery of the level West, after the invention of the railroad, came the Homestead Act of 1862. Under those conditions the wise men of the American Congress in that year declared that 160 acres was a suitable family farm unit. They took the remarkable policy of giving it to anyone who would come and live on it. Canada followed suit. For fifty years we had the world's grandest carnival of free land, at the end of which time all the good farm land was taken up.

## The Felling of the Continent—Waste of Natural Resources

How did this theory work with regard to maintaining our stock of natural resources? The answer is: it produced almost unbelievable wastes.

Take forests, for example. In the eastern half of the United States the riches of lumber were completely unrivaled in any large area of the world. Here was good timber, including the prized cypress in the swamps beside the Gulf of Mexico and the matchless white pine of New England and the Great Lakes. This timber land was given away on the same conditions as farm land. In the Lake Region, for example, timber land was handed out in quarter sections like plow land. A quarter section of timber in the midst of a forest is a unit that an owner cannot protect from fire, so the lumberman was almost compelled to let fire follow him and complete the destruction of the forests. This was socially urged on by a foolish system of taxing young forest rather than lumber. As a result of this conspiracy of destruction the land on which stood the magnificent pine forests of Michigan fifty or sixty years ago, was lumbered, burned, burned again and again and yet again, until all the trees were dead and all the humus burned away down to sand. Experts report that it will take five hundred years for nature, beginning with bushes and weed trees, to build up once more the soil and to raise another forest of pine. Therefore states like New York, Pennsylvania, Michigan, once the leaders in lumber production, are now heavy importers. We are using lumber several times as fast as we grow it, and an area of onetime forest as large as Great Britain is classed as waste because of repeated burning.

The waste of petroleum is another completely unpardonable social crime. The mechanical cause of this waste lies in the fact that oil will flow from one man's land to the land of another man. A social cause of this waste is the governmental indiscretion of giving away farms with the mineral rights included. After this the discovery of oil on one farm sets the owners of adjacent lands to digging wells quickly that they may get all the oil they can from this free-flowing pool to which every tract of land above it is a potential gateway. Result: millions wasted in needless wells, and the greater part of the oil that might be secured is left in the ground, because of the wasteful removal of the natural gas which presses it out.[3]

It is in the ownership of farm lands that we find the most amazing breakdown of the theory that a man will take care of what he owns. The waste of soil by gully erosion, sheet erosion, wind erosion is the most unbelievable and most appalling of all our resource wastes. If the soil is left, a forest will eventually come back; we may discover partial substitutes for oil; but land is irreplaceable.

In many localities we appear to have gone at farms with the idea that we will skin this one and get another; move as the lumberman moved, from area to area. This situation has been aggravated by a misfit agriculture transplanted from Europe,[4] a continent whose conditions differ from our own. As to results, I cite three examples. (1) Because of soil destruction, certain counties in Georgia have lost more than half of their rural population; (2)

[3] J. Russell Smith, *Men and Resources,* Harcourt, Brace & Co., 1937, Chapter 1, p. 10, for brief account of waste of natural resources and causes thereof.

[4] J. Russell Smith, *Tree Crops, a Permanent Agriculture,* Chap. 1, Harcourt, Brace & Co.

surveys by the Tennessee Valley Authority show that in the drainage area above the Norris reservoir erosion has destroyed for agricultural use 60 per cent of the land that had been cleared for farms. This destruction has nearly all been done in less than a century; (3) Oklahoma, opened to white settlement only in 1892, appears on the soil erosion maps[5] as one of the most desperately destroyed. No people—civilized, semi-civilized, barbarian, or savage—has ever destroyed soil so rapidly as we have done and are yet doing in the United States—our machines give us greater powers of destruction than the primitives had.

II. HOW HAS THE AMERICAN SYSTEM OF GIVING AWAY NATURAL RESOURCES WORKED TO SUPPLY THE NEEDS OF THE PEOPLE?

The European races have been turned loose in the richest of continents to take, to hold, to own, to buy and sell, to make a profit (cash, immediate, personal), even if wastage and complete destruction of the resources accompanied the process. We have had this unrivaled opportunity of freedom with riches for three centuries, and what is the result? We have already referred to the waste of

[5] Bulletins from the Soil Conservation Service, U. S. Dept. of Agriculture, will give detailed accounts and statistical measures of our soil destruction, and suggestions for its avoidance. The reports of the U. S. National Resources Board of December 1, 1934, and later give fuller accounts. A very brief summary of causes and results is to be had in *Men and Resources*, J. Russell Smith, Harcourt, Brace & Co., 1937.

natural resources; but what has been the result for men? At the end of this three centuries of opportunity, millions are out of a job and cannot find work, regardless of skill, training, good record, and honest effort. Millions are ill clad and cold. Millions are ill sheltered. They want to work. The resources are here. The factories, farms, forests and mines, and even piles of raw material await. But some mysterious bafflement prevents the men and the mechanisms from working to produce the much needed goods. We have devised a system of ownership, private and corporate, of leases, of transportation systems, of business organizations which somehow manage to keep men separated from resources and opportunity.

What is the cause of this frustration? I do not mean to say it is all a matter of natural resources. We must seek the causes in two fields: first, the ownership and control of natural resources—the things made by nature; and, second, the ownership and control of the products of industry—the things made by man. These two great realms of human affairs are dominated by two concepts: for the resources, complete private ownership; for the products of private industry, the profit system. Examine these two for the causes of our trouble.

Certainly the conditions of American economic life today demand the most thorough re-examination of every assumption, every principle, every important practice, because of the *rapid increase in the inefficiency* of our economic system to serve the people. I say its increase in *inefficiency* because, in addition to great natural resources, we are having, year by year, a very rapid increase in the efficiency of machinery. This enables a smaller and ever smaller number of men to produce ever greater and greater quantities of goods. Indeed, during the supposedly prosperous years 1920 to 1929 there was a steady decline in the actual number of persons engaged in the great basic industries of agriculture and manufacturing.[6]

While both profit system and control of resources merit examination, this chapter discusses only the control and use of natural resources.

We have had a swift shift (historically) from common ownership to private ownership. As operated prior to 1929 this private ownership has failed. The period since 1929 has seen swift changes back toward the concept of *public interest*.

How shall this rising concept be made effective?

## III. THE RESTORATION OF THE PUBLIC INTEREST

It is spiritually easy for a sympathetic person with a little leisure to conclude that slums are bad, and that he will do something about it. So we gather our friends together, form an organization which gets groups of slum children together and gives them perhaps a Christmas tree. At this fes-

[6] See publications of the Bureau of Agricultural Economics, U. S. Department of Agriculture, Washington, D. C.

tival a leading industrialist or financier dresses up as Santa Claus and distributes toys and little bags of edibles. In the spring we have a Flower Day for the children, and send them daisies and other spring flowers. We turn an old meeting house into a mission where they can come and play and get a bit of education, during a few hours of the week. We have a Country Week, in which a small proportion of the slum children spend seven or fourteen days in the country. This affords much satisfaction in the breasts of us who make these charitable expressions. *But the young people have spent fifty or fifty-one weeks in the slum. What the slum needs is such reconstruction of society that there will be no inducement to make slums, or, indeed, a society in which slums will be impossible.* Very suggestive in this respect is the study [7] of what has been accomplished at Letchworth (Garden City), Hertfordshire, England, or at Welwyn, another British city scientifically constructed to meet effectively the social as well as the economic needs of man. Suggestive also are the experiments of Henry Ford in distributing manufacturing to villages. [8]

Unfortunately, these interesting cases are only spasmodic examples of conscience and five per cent. Meanwhile whole systems of slum-making forces still stand intrenched in the law and structure of our society and in dearly beloved business prac-

[7] *Letchworth.*
[8] Address Henry Ford, Dearborn, Michigan.

tices. What we need to do is to remove the *causes*. To clean up a few slums and leave the causes untouched is inadequate and stupid. But to *remove causes* involves real change and brings us to the situation described by Laski when he says, "Man's ability to think rationally stops as soon as his economic interests are involved." Therefore it appears that some kind of pressure must be exerted upon those who have control of the earth's resources if we are to restore the concept of the public interest to the point where the resources of this continent can adequately serve the needs of the people.

To awaken and restore public interest in our natural resources invokes no new principle. Already in behalf of the public interest taxes are levied on a great many things, including natural resources. For example, the people of a certain locality conclude that they need a public improvement which requires land. They act through the duly constituted public bodies (counties, cities, states, the national government) to take this land by the public right called eminent domain and use it for a road, a school, a playground, a park, a national forest, or a slum clearance.

The extreme case of action of this sort is the military draft. We conclude that we need to be defended from a foreign enemy. We exercise the right of eminent domain, take a thousand young men, and say, "You must go out and defend us, even though you die." That is war. We need to live more heroically in times of peace.

From this day onward we need among other things the following:

(*a*) *All undiscovered minerals should belong to the public—county, state, or nation.* Let every man who owns mineral declare it, register it with accurate description like any other land ownership, pay taxes on it; otherwise, mineral resources when they appear belong to the state. The idea that private ownership produces efficient use fails most glaringly of all in the ownership of mineral resources. We found, especially with regard to oil, how criminally private ownership wastes a precious, limited, and irreplaceable material.

As to the effects of the sudden wealth that ownership of minerals brings to individuals, I wish that someone would undertake the following sociological study. Go to an oil field ten, fifteen, twenty, or twenty-five years after the discovery of oil had made all the people in a limited area suddenly rich. Get the case histories of these persons and families upon whom the whims of geology and land ownership had brought the fairyland wish of sudden riches. I have heard just enough about it to think that the record of silliness, folly, speculation, poverty, disappointment, disillusion, and debauchery would be a smashing argument against letting people get money that way.

## The Control and Use of Natural Resources

### Source of Revenues

As an easy, burdenless, reasonable, effective source of taxation, what can beat a mineral royalty? Here is a farmer and his wife, contentedly tilling the 160 acre farm, raising sons and daughters, helping to feed and uphold the nation. Comes the discovery of oil. The farm becomes a field of derricks. The farmer family become foolish millionaires. If the government owned the oil, there would be one oil derrick, or perhaps none, and while under present conditions the farm may yield oil for a few years, under the operation of the whole oil field in the public interest there would be a dozen or two wells in a township that might yield oil for a century.

### A Government Oil Field

I have traveled through the oil fields of Trinidad, British West Indies, where oil belongs to the government. Except for good roads and the sight of a refinery and the fairly dense population, I did not know when I entered or left the oil field, the wells were so few and far apart. Although so few and far apart, the wells sufficed to drain the oil in the most economical and efficient manner. The labor and materials spent upon them were but a fraction of that spent in the enormously over-equipped American fields, but the percentage of oil retrieved in the over-equipped American field is but a fraction of that which the few wells will win from the Trinidad fields. Then, too, every barrel of this greater Trinidadian output gives a greater income to the government, because the royalties go to it rather than to the persons who by chance owned the farms. The land owners are left as before in practically undisturbed possession of their land—the surface. The Trinidad field will employ hundreds of people for decades, whereas an American field will employ thousands for a few years. Privately owned oil winds up in large part by belonging to nobody because it is wasted.

Perhaps someone says, "But public ownership of mineral resources will check private initiative in searching for minerals." This applies but faintly to our most important mineral, namely, coal, most of which has long since been discovered. The search for hidden minerals would probably be as successful if made by the geological surveys of the various states and nations as when made by geologists working for private companies. Geologists employed by the private companies were turned off by the scores and hundreds about 1930 or 1931, pathetically seeking almost any kind of employment.

Government ownership would greatly aid in planning the more efficient use of minerals in many ways. For example, for a few decades South Carolina dug up and feverishly exported phosphate rock. Now she is importing it from Florida. Florida is now shipping it hither and yon but in a few decades will probably begin to import it from some other place.

(*b*) *Property taxes should be based upon natural resources and not upon improvements.*

This is sometimes called the Single Tax, a term much associated with the name of Henry George, who expounded it so clearly more than half a century ago. The present system of land ownership by individuals in United States and Canada is a kind of private monopoly. We pay a lot of money to get possession, and we may or may not use the land. The owner may hold his land out of use to make others pay for it. If the natural-resource value of land were taxed to the full extent, that is to say, if the government took the whole monopoly value, there would be no advantage in holding land except to use it, and this would probably result in a great freeing of natural resources, so that they could be more fully utilized. One of the great handicaps of the unemployed is that they cannot get a chance to work the land.

If we were to shift our attention from self-interest and the pleasure of monopoly control, and think instead of the welfare of society, it would be hard to find objections to the use of this tax on natural resources as a joint means of raising revenue and increasing business opportunity. Perhaps it would go far towards realizing the ideal (or right) that is stated in these words of George Higgins, Melbourne, Australia: *"Economic Justice* would give each child, as it arrives in the world, the right of access to, and the use of, natural resources, on terms of equality with all living human beings. Monopoly of natural resources is not consistent with economic justice, because they are limited in volume, and are the only sources from which successive generations can obtain for themselves the necessaries of life. Economists use the word 'land' to embrace all natural resources.

"Each individual is entitled to possess what he or she by his or her labour produces, such possessions including the right to use or exchange products as may be desired."

The settlement of the Matanuska Valley in Alaska illustrates very effectively the way our present system interferes with land use. Some scores of families on relief rolls were gathered up in north central United States, and at government expense transported to the Pacific coast, thence to Alaska, where the government helped them build houses on government homesteads. There, in this remote place under the shadow of the Arctic mountains, close to the Arctic Circle, these people set out to make their livings. Gravely we sent them, gravely they went, at our great expense. It appears that our land system has robbed us of our proper sense of humor, for at that moment there was more unused land in Cook County, Illinois (Chicago), than these settlers took in far away Alaska with all its limitations.

In various parts of the United States many scores of communities are struggling to form self-help co-operatives whereby the unemployed can work for the unemployed. But one of the first things they want is land, the vital, the fundamental, the irreplaceable resource. Land should be freed, so that it may be used.

(c) *To face the problems of farm tenancy and farm ownership.*

In a recently published two-volume study of North America a European scholar[9] says that we have in our share-croppers of the Cotton Belt a body of persons whose plight is worse than that of any similar mass of people in Europe.

This cotton share-cropper system seems to be one in which the land owner sets out to skin the tenant; the tenant sets out to skin the land owner; the neighborhood gets skinned; the farm gets thoroughly skinned (often destroyed by erosion[10]) ; and all this in one of the most potentially productive areas of the world.

Many of the fine farming sections of the Middle West are in the process of swift shift from the one-family 160 acre farm to a big mechanized farm or to a string of chain farms operated by one manager. I have in mind a case in Illinois where seventeen farms, under different ownerships, are managed by one young college graduate, who supervises the tenants, plans, buys, and sells for them.

We are doing nothing about these things except

---

[9] Baulig, A. B., *North America.*
[10] Goodrich, Carter and others, *Migration and Economic Opportunity,* University of Pennsylvania Press, 1936.

to make a few reports and here and there to raise a plaintive cry. We haven't faced the question at all as to what land is for. We need to re-examine our assumptions in this swiftly changing era of mechanized economics. Is land to be used solely to make dividends, and therefore to be operated purely on a financial basis, or is it to support a way of life and a type of society? Messrs. Hitler and Mussolini are controlling it very vigorously to maintain a type of society—one that will provide infantrymen and national self-sufficiency.

The Danes also have decided that land is to support a type of society. They prefer to proceed to get a ten or twenty acre farm with its owner upon it, in preference to an 80 acre farm or an 800 acre farm with an owner and several tenants or farm hands. Therefore the Danes have passed laws prohibiting a man from purchasing his neighbor's farm, with the result that Denmark is having greater and greater subdivision of the land, more and more land owners, and tenancy has almost disappeared because the farms are not big enough for tenants. This may produce some increase in cost of production. However, that may be an open question, but in any case the Danes know what they want and have the courage to create it. Apparently we do not yet even know what we want.

The British have a longstanding tenant system, in which the possession of a lease is almost the same as ownership. Men stay for decades, pass the farm on from generation to generation. They take good care of the land and maintain it and the community as though they were land owners. A successful British farmer with whom I spent a day flouted the idea of wishing to own land. "Why!" said he, "to buy land I would have to go to the bank and pay five per cent for the money. Lord So-and-so, the owner of this farm, is only getting two and a half per cent. I don't want to own land. I'm a good farmer and can lease all I want."

(*d*) *Develop and act upon the trusteeship concept of land ownership.*

I am now personally free to go out and buy land, misuse it, gully it, let it wash away and ruin it; buy forest and let the fire run through it, kill the trees, burn the earth. This I should not be permitted to do. We need to develop in people's minds the idea that they do not own land outright; they have it in a sense of trusteeship. No one *owns* his desk in a school, nor does he own a place in the public road while passing along it. No more should the individual be allowed to gully and injure land than he should be allowed to take his exercise by digging holes in the public highway.

(*e*) *Establish transport control in the interests of the wise use of resources and the socially effective distribution of wealth.*

Our railroads were built and operated for profit. Their main objective was that of earning dividends for the investor. Their service to the public was an incidental. It has been truly said that to the railroad company we have left the decision of what fields should become a village; what villages should become towns, what towns should become cities, what cities should become metropolises. For example, by the basing-point system of rate making which prevails in the southeastern part of the United States, the rate from Chicago to a town north of Atlanta, Georgia, on the route between Chicago and Atlanta, is the freight rate from Chicago to Atlanta, and from Atlanta back to that town. This means that Atlanta has a great business and commercial advantage over thousands of square miles of territory around it. The American railway rate system gives a business advantage to a few points. There businesses must gather. There also people must gather despite the fact that their numbers make cities and metropolises with their innumerable disadvantages in the development of normal, wholesome society, and a wholesome life for boys and girls, men and women.

*The railway rate system should be rearranged in the interest of the public welfare.* Someone cries out in horror, "Would you disarrange American industry?" In my answer I would call attention to the fact that in war we disarrange men's lives to the point of drafting them and killing them. In peace we need to do more drafting of property. If we did this the peace would be easier to keep. Here is a transport system full of evils. Because change will rearrange business, shall we sit down and calmly accept the evil forever? Or shall we adopt a policy which may be expected to remove the evils—gradually perhaps, but surely?

## IV. RESOURCES IN INTERNATIONAL RELATIONS

We hear much talk these days about the fact that certain nations do not have an abundant supply of raw materials; that there should be a redistribution of raw materials. The need is real but much of this talk is very silly. To see how silly it is, one should notice that almost without exception people of all countries can buy any and all of the easily transportable raw materials at the same price. Japan, Italy, England, Iceland pay the same price for American cotton, Canadian paper, Swedish ore, Venezuelan oil, Malayan rubber, Swedish steel. The prime troublemaker here is not so much the unequal distribution of raw materials as it is *the closing of markets.*

If a man lives on an unproductive rock—say, Manhattan Island—he can get along very well by buying his water, his food, his raw materials, provided he can on this bare rock manufacture these things into some salable product and then sell it and get money to buy more materials. The same thing is true of Japan, of Italy, of Germany, the three who cry out the most about the scarcity of raw materials. They all have difficulty in buying our American cotton because we have put up tariffs making it difficult for them to send in goods to pay for the cotton. Other countries have followed our iniquitous example, and we have had this last quarter of a century the most marvelous and idiotic tariff race, each nation vying with the others to see how high it can put tariffs, how many more restrictions it can make in the matter of quotas and embargoes—how much more it can increase the cost of living within its own borders.[11]

A committee of the League of Nations has predicted that the tariff mania may result in wholesale starvation of large masses of people. Germany in 1937 is not far from it.

This tariff craze arises in part from a desire for military strength, but in large part from the influence of scarcity economics.[12]

We see scarcity economics very plainly in the following cases:

(1) The idea that goods may be had cheaply in foreign countries terrifies us.

(2) The Cotton Belt of the United States shivers to think what will happen if a cotton-picking machine relieves ten million people of three months' hard work every autumn.

(3) We actually pay hundreds of millions of dollars a year to support prisoners in idleness and the moral degeneration that idleness produces, rather than let them make goods which would be worth billions.

We can probably do but little with the easing up

[11] In this connection, examine the world regions map in footnote 3, above.

[12] *Methods of Achieving Economic Justice,* pamphlet, Friends Central Bureau, 1515 Cherry Street, Philadelphia, Pa.

of international tensions arising from resource situations until we have done something to abolish the grip that scarcity economics has upon our minds. Certainly there is small prospect of the rich nations voluntarily handing over to the poor nations shiploads of resources at less than cost, or ceding them areas of land. The best hope is to abolish scarcity economics, and the reduction of tariffs is a good place to start.

A great help in that direction will be the spread of the knowledge of a simple mathematical discovery which by some psychological mystery still seems to remain largely a secret. The mathematical fact is that the world's exports and imports do actually balance. They *must* do so. They cannot help doing so. The citizens of the United States ship, let us say, $1,000,000 worth of merchandise to the citizens of France. The correct statistical record is: United States exports $1,000,000—French imports $1,000,000. The balance is perfect, and a million transactions would not change it. These things are unknown to the legislative mind at Washington. The legislative record shows that the great American virtue in foreign trade, as shown by legislative acts, is to export—export but do not import. In national policy we stick to it with all the persistence of a dumb animal driven by a blind instinct. In fact, that is just what it is, a blind instinct produced by the atmosphere of scarcity economics.

After the World War the nations of Europe tried to send to the United States some billions of dollars' worth of goods they owed us (war debts). We put up our tariffs in horror and refused to receive the goods.

*Conclusion.* In this troubled hour of feverish rearmament, the good citizen should devote much of his leisure to the study of economic questions. *If he does this with the realization that his welfare lies in being one of a prosperous people rather than in having special privileges,* he will probably want to strengthen the forces that compel conservation of natural resources; make many changes in taxation looking towards improving society as well as raising revenue, such as taxing unearned increment of land values 100 per cent; create a farm tenant system that provides permanency approaching ownership; revise the railway rate structure to provide for better distribution of industries and people over the United States: abolish a host of tariffs so that people can trade for raw materials rather than fight for them; and finally he will work to create a system of distribution of the produce of industry in which the rewards will go to those who create abundance rather than (as now) to those who create scarcity.

# XI

## THE PROBLEM OF CRIME

### S. B. Laughlin, Ph.D.
###### Professor of Sociology and Anthropology, Willamette University

DO you love one another as becomes the followers of Christ? Are you careful of the reputation of others? When differences arise, do you make earnest efforts to end them speedily?

Do you observe simplicity in your manner of living? Are you careful to live within your income and avoid involving yourselves in business beyond your ability to manage? Are you just in your dealings, punctual to your promises, prompt in the payment of your debts and free from defrauding the public revenue?

### I

As the problem of crime is fundamentally one of causation, the purpose of this paper is to explain the causes of crime and lawlessness in the United States and particularly why our crime rate is the highest in the civilized world.

Crime is the violation of the law. Therefore, a crime is a technical term purely arbitrary and manmade. If the law punishing murder were repealed one person might kill another in cold blood and not

253

be a criminal. It is then obvious that no one can be a born criminal and that the commission of a crime is not the result of an instinct.

J. Edgar Hoover tells us that there are 3,500,000 criminals actively at work in the United States; that 1,500,000 felonies are committed each year and that there are 700,000 convicts behind prison bars. He also estimates the annual cost of crime to be $15,000,000,000. This is $120 per person or $600 for a family of five.

According to Frederick Hoffman, our leading crime statistician, the homicide rate of the United States in 1933 was 10.7 per 100,000 population, while that of England and Wales in 1932 was 0.5. The rates for other European countries, mostly for 1930 or 1931, were as follows: Netherlands 0.5, Norway 1, Scotland 1, France 1, Spain 1, Portugal 2, Switzerland 2, Germany 2, Austria 3, Czechoslovakia 3, Greece 5, Estonia 6.

### HOMICIDE RATES FOR AMERICAN CITIES
#### (Per 100,000 Population)

| TEN LARGEST CITIES | | TEN LEADING CITIES | |
|---|---|---|---|
| St. Louis | 16.8 | Lexington | 59.5 |
| Cleveland | 15.4 | Little Rock | 52.5 |
| Chicago | 14.2 | Memphis | 50.8 |
| Baltimore | 8.6 | Birmingham | 49.5 |
| Pittsburgh | 8.5 | Atlanta | 47.6 |
| Los Angeles | 7.6 | Jacksonville | 47.4 |
| Detroit | 7.4 | Macon | 44.4 |
| New York | 7.4 | Montgomery | 41.5 |
| Philadelphia | 6.7 | Savannah | 39.7 |
| Boston | 4.0 | Nashville | 36.4 |

TEN FOREIGN CITIES

| | | | | | |
|---|---|---|---|---|---|
| Leningrad ... | 1924-29 | 9.9 | Berlin ....... | 1921-30 | 1.8 |
| Rio de Janeiro | 1921-28 | 7.5 | Melbourne ... | 1921-30 | 1.6 |
| Moscow ..... | 1924-28 | 4.9 | Tokyo ....... | 1920-29 | 0.9 |
| Rome ....... | 1921-30 | 4.4 | London ..... | 1921-30 | 0.8 |
| Vienna ...... | 1921-30 | 2.7 | Amsterdam .. | 1921-30 | 0.3 |

The above figures justify his statement that "our homicide death rate is by far the highest for any civilized country in the world."

At this point someone may remark that our high rate is due to the foreign born. A study of the figures given above will show that the highest rates are all in southern cities where the number of foreign born is the lowest. Roger Babson says, "Statistics even show that crime has increased as immigration has decreased."

Alida C. Bowles in the Wickersham report on *Crime and the Foreign Born* draws the following conclusions:

(1) That in proportion to their respective numbers the foreign born commit considerably fewer crimes than the native born.

(2) That the foreign born approach the record of the native whites most closely in the commission of crimes involving personal violence.

(3) That in crimes for gain (including robbery, in which there is also personal violence or threat of violence) the native whites greatly exceed the foreign born.

(4) That there is insufficient information available to warrant any deduction as to criminal activ-

255

ity among the native born of foreign parentage as compared with those of native parentage.

If the first generation are more criminal than their parents that fact would prove that we admit law-abiding peasants of Europe and by our bad environment make criminals out of their children. Every generation of Americans from Benjamin Franklin to the present has complained about the criminality of the foreigners. Perhaps the Indians have always felt that every wave of immigration from Europe was a crime wave or rather a tidal inundation of lawlessness.

In his Pennsylvania colony, William Penn applied the Quaker principles of brotherly love and treated the Indians with the respect that is due from one of God's creatures to another. The result was that for seventy years, or while the Penn influence remained, there was no conflict between whites and Indians. Voltaire said that Penn's treaty with the Indians was the only treaty between these people and the Christians not ratified by an oath and that was never broken.

II

Any discussion of the causes of crime and lawlessness in the United States must take into consideration the character of the early colonists. For this purpose they may be divided into three classes:

(1) The land-hungry, discontented, restless and adventurous of Europe in revolt against "status."

(2) Non-conformists in religion.

(3) Convicts and indentured servants.

When feudalism and the Catholic Church were in their prime in Europe, from Norman days to the end of the Crusades, society was relatively static and might be divided into three classes: the peasant to obey and serve; the noble to fight and rule; the priest to instruct and pray. Every man was taught to be content to remain in the station in life in which he was born. "Let every man abide in the same calling wherein he was called" was a well-heeded text.

With the break up of feudalism, the rise of cities, commerce and money economy, there arose another class that did not fit into the status of the three classes mentioned above. This was the bourgeois or business man. This new middle class became the backbone of the Calvinistic or Puritan element in the Reformation. Following the Reformation there was developed the theory of the natural and inherent rights of man as limitations upon social organization and the powers of government. This was a complete abandonment of the social concepts of the feudal system which was based upon interrelated duties of service and protection.

It was also a challenge to the claims of absolutism then maintained by the Stuart kings. Finally the powers of the Crown were limited; the independence of the judiciary was recognized; the supremacy of the people through parliament was established; and the foundations were laid for the gradual development, through the processes of orderly evolution, of the cohesive and highly flexible national organization of modern England. The original colonies were established in America during this period of transition, of social unrest and conflict which culminated in the Revolutions of 1649 and 1688.

Three things thus characterized the early colonists: economic discontent; religious non-conformity; and a political theory that emphasized rights rather than duties, coupled with the belief that each individual was vested with the right to decide what laws he would or would not obey.

For instance, the Massachusetts Company violated the law by bringing the charter with them but even then the terms of the charter were not complied with. As James Truslow Adams says: "The way in which those supposedly godly persons, the leaders of the Massachusetts theocracy, began at once by breaking the laws of England will help us to an understanding of the whole colonial situation." And as Henry W. Anderson of the Wickersham Commission says, "It may be said with truth that the American social organization came into existence animated by a spirit of revolution and characterized by acts of lawlessness."

It is not necessary or possible to say much about the colonial convicts and indentured servants. The total number was probably several thousand. Many English convicts were given their choice between being hanged or going to the colonies. Apparently they all preferred the New World. However it should be said that most of their crimes were not what we should consider serious.

There were also many indentured servants who were naturally from the lower classes. Some were of good stock but no doubt many were poor material for the building of a new nation.

Of the non-English elements, the Dutch, the Germans, the French Huguenots, and the Scotch-Irish, none were in sympathy with the English form of government, and the Scotch-Irish were particularly bitter toward England because of many injustices at her hands.

### III

The old pun that when the early colonists landed upon the wild New England shore they fell upon their knees and then upon the aborigines very pungently expresses the truth. The Puritans likened themselves to the Israelites entering the land of Canaan, a chosen people commissioned by God to exterminate the natives—men, women, and children.

A few references will illustrate this point. In the Pequot War, John Mason surrounded the Indians in their village, set it on fire, and shot down the natives as they fled. When Cotton Mather heard of the massacre, he entered his pulpit and thanked God that "on this day, we have sent six hundred heathen souls to hell." Underhill, who had taken part in the massacre, said, "Sometimes the Scripture declareth women and children must perish with their parents. We had sufficient light from the word of God for our proceedings." The General Court offered a bounty for Indian scalps, irrespective of sex or age. "Colonel John Washington, first of that great name in American history, violated in 1673 not only the most solemn engagement of his people, but ignored a flag of truce and murdered a group of Indian prisoners not far from the site of the present Capitol of the United States . . ." (quoted from William E. Dodd). The American motto has been, "The only good Indian is a dead Indian." The boyhood ambition of many an American has been to go out west and shoot an Indian.

Anyone who reads Helen Hunt Jackson's *A Century of Dishonor* will realize that the American people and their government, with few exceptions, have shown a wanton and ruthless disregard for the life and property of the Indian.

Colonial smuggling can best be described in the words of Professor Dodd: "The British Government enacted the most stringent trade regulations designed to control the commerce of the vast no man's region, the South Atlantic Ocean. Not a colony, north or south, but violated these laws regularly and purposely for a whole century before the birth of the United States. In South Carolina, in Maryland, and in Massachusetts it was a common saying in 1700, as in 1776, that Colonial juries would not convict men who ignored maritime law;

and all the world knew that the President of the Continental Congress just before the outbreak of the Revolution was a notorious smuggler of goods into Boston."

According to the Calvinistic concept of salvation the Christian must work so fast that the devil cannot catch him. The purpose of the work was to accumulate wealth as an evidence of God's favor. Prosperity was then the proof of goodness; economic failure was a sign of God's displeasure. Money-making became a moral virtue and "developing" the country a patriotic duty.

Thus was laid the foundation of the gospel of materialism which is a basic cause of crime in the United States. The origin of such a concept is found in the Old Testament where the Hebrew makes a bargain with God. The contract runs as follows: God, the party of the first part, will furnish sunshine, rain and good crops; man, the party of the second part, will worship Him and give Him a tenth of all the increase.

Furthermore Calvin enjoined servants to obey their masters without rebellion. This has tended to produce a docile laboring class and is used to justify the employing classes in their dominance of the economic order.

Coupled with the above philosophy of work was its corollary, the aversion to play or pleasure. Someone has said that the Puritans objected to bear-baiting not because of the pain it gave the bear but because of the pleasure it gave to the spectators.

The common colonial attitude toward play can best be expressed by stating the position of the Methodist Church in regard to students in its schools in 1792: "We prohibit *Play* in the strongest terms. . . . The students shall be indulged in nothing which the world calls *Play*. Let this rule be observed with the strictest nicety; for those who play when they are young, will play when they are old."

Urbanization with the consequent idleness of city children has shown us the high correlation between the lack of playgrounds and juvenile delinquency. Whenever attempts are made to secure adequate recreational facilities the old perverted attitude toward the useful purpose of play and recreation has reasserted itself like a specter from the past, to hamper such attempts.

In the eighteenth century John Wesley saw the dilemma of Puritan philosophy. He wrote, "I fear whenever riches have increased, the essence of religion has decreased in the same proportion. Therefore I do not see how it is possible in the nature of things for any revival of true religion to continue long. For religion must necessarily produce both industry and frugality, and these cannot but produce riches. But as riches increase, so will pride, anger, and love of the world in all its branches. . . . Is there no way to prevent people from being diligent and frugal; must we exhort all Christians to gain all they can and to save all they can; that is,

in effect, to grow rich." But he also encouraged
Christians to give all they could.

John Woolman broke the vicious circle that
John Wesley propounded. When his business had
reached a certain stage he had a stoppage in his
mind against its further expansion. He even re-
duced his business operations and spent the re-
mainder of his life fighting slavery. Friends are
again pioneering in the field of economic justice.

The Calvinistic and the Quaker philosophies of
life, in general, and of God and man in particular,
are poles apart and cannot be reconciled. Calvinistic theology is a hard, stern, legalistic affair based
on the Old Testament. According to it, "All children have wicked hearts when they are born: and
that makes them so wicked, when they grow up
into life. Even little infants, that appear so innocent and pretty, are God's little enemies at heart."
(Quoted in Fleming, *Children and Puritanism*.)
This repression of the child leads to all kinds of
pathological results. Man is clay in the hands of
the potter. Women and colored races are inferior.
Salvation is assured by financial success. It makes
for a fatalistic, mechanistic and materialistic conception of life. The Calvinist will be a capitalist
but not a pacifist.

Quakerism is the gospel of brotherly love and is
based on the teachings of Jesus. According to it,
every child is created in the image of God with a
spark of divinity in its soul and is innocent and
guiltless until it reaches the age of accountability.

It then has freedom of will to follow or reject this "Inner Light."

Here is the heart of a vital problem. If we take the words of Jesus seriously we will find no support to the idea that a Christian should strive to become rich. On the contrary, He says that life does not consist in the abundance of one's possessions. "For what shall it profit a man if he gain the whole world and lose his own soul?" "It is easier for a camel to pass through the eye of a needle, than for a rich man to enter into the kingdom of God."

The more abundant life is spiritual and not material. This, of course, does not mean that reasonable attention should not be given to meeting material needs.

The Christian, striving to live the more abundant life, will find many things more important to do than to accumulate money. He will agree with Aristotle that the best state of society is the one where there are neither rich nor poor. Such a condition would certainly remove many occasions for crime.

It is a strange paradox, difficult to explain, that the Puritans, who left England to escape persecution for conscience sake should in turn persecute even unto death those who differed from them.

The banishment of Roger Williams and Anne Hutchinson, the hanging of four Quakers, and the execution of twenty-nine alleged witches, as well as religious persecutions in Virginia and New York, all in the name of God, helped develop a certain phase of lawlessness that later manifested itself in the persecution of the Mormons, Catholics, and Jews.

Friends have never shown a persecuting spirit. Prior to the Revolution, Friends exerted a strong influence in five of the thirteen original colonies—Pennsylvania, New Jersey, Delaware, Rhode Island and North Carolina. They were all noted for religious liberty.

### IV

The most ominous event of all the lawless acts preceding the actual outbreak of the American Revolution was the Boston Tea Party of December 16, 1773. The tax on tea was particularly obnoxious to the colonial merchants and they had resorted to smuggling on a large scale in order to avoid it and get tea cheaper.

The British Government then remitted the tax previously paid by the East India Company and permitted it to import tea directly. This tea could then have been sold cheaper than the smuggled tea. The merchants did not want to meet this competition, so they made an alliance with the mob and destroyed $90,000 worth of property. Benjamin Franklin felt the injustice of the act so keenly that he offered to reimburse the company out of his own pocket. The merchants of Philadelphia met and passed a resolution that the act was a wanton destruction of property and that the perpetrators ought to be made to pay for it. The whole story has been told to each generation of Americans in such a distorted way that they have come to glory in an act of deliberate lawlessness and wanton destruction of property.

Authorities agree that at the outbreak of the Revolution the colonists were divided into three groups. One-third favored rebellion, one-third were indifferent, and one-third were loyal to the government. During the Revolution, or soon after its close, at least 100,000 of these loyalists were officially expelled or forced to leave the country.

Massachusetts expelled by name 308 of her leading citizens, 60 of whom were graduates of Harvard College. Van Tyne says, "It is not unlikely that the early errors of the republic in finance, diplomacy, and politics might have been in part corrected by the conservative element exiled." Keenleyside says, "Thus, the United States at the very outset of its independent career lost close to 100,000 of its most reputable and conservative citizens. It may be argued that this loss has been a powerful contributing factor in producing that disrespect for law and tendency toward mob action which have occasionally characterized American society."

Parrington says, "The disruption of colonial society resulting from the expulsion of the Loyalists was far graver than we commonly assume. Shiploads of excellent gentlemen, and among them the most cultivated minds in America, were driven from their firesides and sent forth to seek new homes. . . ." The change of temper that came over American society with the loss of the Loyalists was immense and far-reaching. For the first time the middle class was free to create a civilization after its own ideals. Dignity and culture were to count for less and assertiveness for more. Ways became less leisurely, the social temper less urbane. The charm of the older aristocracy disappeared along with its indisputable evils. A franker evaluation of success in terms of money began to obscure the older personal and family distinctions."

Becker says, "With the British troops there sailed away a great company of Loyalist exiles, never to return; part of the thousands who renounced their heritage and their country in defense of political and social ideals that belonged to the past. America thus lost the service of many men of ability, of high integrity, and of genuine culture: clergymen and scholars, landowners and merchants of substantial estate, men learned in the law, high officials of proved experience in politics and administration. The great achievements of history have their price; and American independence was won only by the sacrifice of much that was best in colonial society. Something fine and amiable in manner, something charming in customs, much that was most excellent in the traditions of politics and public morality disappeared with the ruin of those who thought themselves, and often were in fact, 'of the better sort.' "

Probably 60,000 of these Loyalists went to Canada. Their influence there can best be expressed in the words of Waugh: "Nearly all of the advantages of Canada today in law, education, and morals are due largely to the United Empire Loyalist's ancestry. Respect for law, obedience to the government, attachment to the Church, and loyalty to the empire were the outstanding characteristics of early Canada."

The failure of our history books to tell us the facts of our lawless heritage, as outlined above, has been one factor in the perpetuation of that heritage. It will probably come as a surprise to many and a shock to some to learn that Sir William Franklin, son of Benjamin Franklin, served as a British officer in New Jersey during the Revolution.

V

By the time the American people had started upon their independent career as the United States of America, disrespect for law as such was a well established attitude and mob violence was the customary reaction to real or fancied grievances. In other words, the seeds of future crime were already planted.

Additional instances of violation of law will serve to illustrate the nature of our lawless heritage.

From the time of Washington to Jackson the illegal slave trade continued. The rights of the

Indians to life and property were violated as usual.

Politics in the North became unfashionable; and to a large extent, for many years, men of wealth and refinement kept out of political life.

Marcy of New York invented the famous phrase: "To the victors belong the spoils." President Jackson originated the practice of rotation in office when, in one of his messages, he said, "The duties of all public offices are, or at least admit of being made, so plain and simple that men of intelligence may readily qualify themselves for their peformance; and I cannot but believe that more is lost by the long continuance of men in office than is generally to be gained by their experience."

The tradition of efficient and unselfish devotion to public service has never developed in the United States. From that time to the present there has been an unbroken record of graft and corruption in public life.

An ominous change in the nature of crime took place about 1830. Previously to that time almost all our law breaking had to do with business transactions, but thereafter there developed another phase —violence against the person.

Beginning in 1834 and continuing until the 1850's there were a number of popular outbreaks against the Irish Catholics. In 1834 the Ursuline Convent near Boston was sacked and burned. In St. Louis the riots were so severe that there were ten resulting deaths. This wave of public lawlessness swept over the country in a nation-wide emotional orgy that left the police forces utterly helpless.

After about fifteen years of intermittent persecution, mob violence against the Mormons reached its culmination at Nauvoo, Illinois, in 1844, when a mob took Joseph Smith and his brother Hyram out of jail and shot them.

The years from 1834 to 1853 were fateful for the Abolitionists, for throughout the country there swept a movement of mob violence intended to silence them by terror. Between 1834 and 1840 there was hardly a place of any size in the North where an Abolitionist could speak with certain safety.

In October, 1835, a mob led by the most prominent citizens of the town broke up an anti-slavery meeting in Montpelier, Vermont. On the same day, another at Utica, New York, with a member of Congress and a county judge at its head, dispersed a meeting of the National Abolition Society.

The Fugitive Slave Law of 1850 helped turn northern sentiment against slavery. In 1851 Theodore Parker said in a sermon that citizens were morally bound to violate the law and that it was a false idea that the people are morally bound to obey any law until it is repealed.

Just before the Civil War the Supreme Court had solemnly enjoined upon citizens the duty of obeying the law. Abraham Lincoln in speaking of the same law said: "I look upon that enactment not as law, but as a violence; it is maintained in violence, and is being executed in violence."

Carl Russell Fish says: "It was significant that, while in the thirties the mobs in the North had attacked the Abolitionists, in the fifties they attacked the United States officers engaged in returning fugitive slaves. . . . The use of force became a common method of advancing causes and of enforcing public opinion. It was viewed with tolerance, was often resorted to by the most respected members of the community, and was often successful. This customary appeal from lawful to illegal and physical methods must be reckoned with as among the significant tendencies of the period. . . . It was ominous that a generation so stirred by profound emotions was also to a considerable degree lawless and given to violence. In the West the pioneer spirit pervaded society, firearms were commonly carried, and law was little observed if it were contrary to the public wish. In the North the 'Underground Railroad' was legally criminal, yet was conducted by the most respectable men and women."

Friends were active in helping Negroes escape from slavery, and Levi Coffin, a Friend, was called the President of the "Underground Railroad." But Friends never violated man-made laws for their own financial gain or glory. They have always held, however, that they must obey God rather than man, even to financial loss. In this instance their conscience, illumined by the Inner Light, directed them to put the human right of a fellow-man for freedom above the property rights of their earthly masters. It was the same spirit that prompted Peter to say, "We must obey God rather than man."

## VI

In the westward march from the Mississippi to the Pacific, there was the usual disregard for the rights of the Indian, and also disregard for the rights of the Spaniard and the Mexican. The slave-holding aristocracy of the South, realizing that cotton was depleting their soil and that the North was gaining additional strength in Congress from the Northwest, began to encroach upon the rights of the Mexicans in Texas. Finally they took the whole Southwest.

A rather ironical explanation of this movement was that the Americans were expanding the area of freedom by extending the boundary of slavery. There is no attempt here to give details of the westward movement but this list of slogans explains the general attitude of mind during that period: *manifest destiny, geographical predestination, the mission of regeneration, natural growth, the white man's burden, paramount interest,* etc. The political philosophy embodied in these phrases may be summed up in the suggestion of Professor Burgess, who said that a native or a less civilized people has no rights to the soil and its resources which a more highly civilized people are bound to respect; and that, if such a people did not submit peacefully, the latter should exterminate them by force.

Very early in the colonial period, as soon as the tidewater region was comparatively well settled, many indentured servants broke their contracts and ran away to unsettled lands on the frontier. These and other settlers of various kinds kept the frontier fringe moving westward usually just a little ahead of the regular branches of orderly government. There was always a certain amount of lawlessness attending this expansion westward, but the most spectacular phase of frontier crime began with the gold rush to California.

The gambling spirit that accompanies gold and silver mining either attracted or developed a type of robbers, bandits, or highwaymen that preyed upon the miners and kept a record of their killings by notches cut on the butts of their revolvers. The bitterness of reconstruction days during the aftermath of the Civil War contributed its share to the frontier bad men.

As the miners were followed by the cattle-men and they in turn were followed by the sheep-men and the farmers followed both, there developed triangular feuds. Cattle stealing, or rustling, became a lucrative form of crime. The cattle kings looked with scorn upon the lowly sheep herders. Sheep ruined the pasture for cattle. Cattle men and shepherds fought the farmer who plowed up the range and ruined the business of both.

The loss of life and property in these bitter feuds has never been computed. When the outlaws became too bad and the towns were of sufficient size vigilante committees of leading citizens took the law into their own hands, hung a few bad men, and drove the rest out of town.

The manner in which western timber lands and the oil resources have fallen into the hands of a relatively few timber and oil barons is another chapter in crime. The method however was more subtle than that of the hold-up man, and the victim was more likely to be the general public. In other words, the government was defrauded. The people, because their pocket was not directly affected, did not express their indignation in direct action.

The disputed possession of gold, silver, cattle, sheep, farm lands, timber lands, oil, and water have caused much loss of life and property. The well known Friends' query: "Are you free from defrauding the public revenue?" has developed a type of citizen who has a high sense of devotion to public duty.

VII

It is perhaps true that the racial heterogeneity of the American people has been a cause of race prejudice which in turn has been a fruitful cause of crime. Due to a certain type of theology the British had a special antipathy toward the Indians.

Two strains of Old Testament theology combined to make both slavery and the long train of evils that followed in its wake: the profit motive and the white man's superiority complex.

## The Problem of Crime

When in 1619 a Dutch ship sailed into the harbor of Jamestown with African Negroes to be sold as slaves no one foresaw that this element in our population would be the occasion for much human misery, violence, war, and bitter racial hatred.

When the Fathers of the Constitution in 1787 said that all men are created equal and then compromised with their consciences by recognizing slavery (and even the slave trade), they fashioned another link in a long chain of crime and violence.

During the colonial period New England shipowners carried on a profitable but illegal trade. They bought molasses in the West Indies, made it into rum, sold the rum in Africa for slaves, then sold the slaves to Southern slave holders. The slave trade was illegal after 1808 but flourished until the Civil War.

When Eli Whitney invented the cotton gin in 1793 he unwittingly made the Civil War a practical certainty. The economic and social results of the cotton gin were not realized until forty years later. By that time the South saw that slavery was profitable and that the tariff gave the manufacturing North an economic advantage. In the meantime it was seen in the North that slavery was not profitable and their more humanitarian leaders were developing a conscience in the matter and were attacking slavery as an evil.

In order to meet this attack the leaders in the South, especially the ministers of the gospel, began to rationalize the justification for slavery and searched the Scriptures for texts to establish this justification.

In 1851, there was published in Louisville, Kentucky, a notable book called the *Bible Defense of Slavery*. It was apparently quite popular, for a sixth edition was printed in 1859. The thesis of this book was that slavery is a divine institution. Its beginning was when Ham, a son of Noah, created black by a fiat of Divine Will, was condemned forever to be the slave of his white brother.

Passages from the Bible, selected all the way from that part of the tenth commandment which says, "Thou shalt not covet thy neighbor's slave," to the advice of the apostle Paul to Onesimus, the run-away slave, that he should return to his master Philemon, and that all slaves should be obedient to their masters, were used to build up the argument that the Bible not only sanctions slavery but even commands it.

Thus fortified by such proof as texts from the Bible, the leaders of the South took the position that slavery was a divine institution and therefore must not be questioned by anyone or even discussed. One young man in a slave state was expelled from college for reading *Uncle Tom's Cabin*.

Therefore as a result of such teaching many Southerners are even today firmly convinced that Negroes are inferior beings.

The social and economic upheaval caused by the Civil War intensified the feeling of racial superiority which from time to time breaks forth in crimes of violence and in the steady denial to the Negro of his constitutional rights.

The most brutalizing and spectacular of all such crimes is that of lynching. This is one method employed by the whites to "keep the Negro in his place." Lynching has been upheld, justified, and even committed by men of prominence and leadership.

The most biting comment on the lynching situation was contained in a newspaper cartoon some years ago. The cartoonist pictured a Turk sitting cross-legged holding in one hand a curved scimitar with blood dripping from one end which spelled out the word "Armenia." In the other hand he held an American newspaper with the word "Lynching" in bold headlines at the top. Out of his mouth was coming this comment, "Almost thou persuadest me to be a Christian."

In recent years crimes of violence in the South are increasing against the share-croppers, both white and black, who are organizing to better their condition. There are 8,500,000 of these people who are worse off than the poorest peasants of Europe.

There is a virulent malady in the world today called Nordicism. It consists in the belief that the blue-eyed blondes, with dolichocephalic heads, who originated around the Baltic Sea, comprise a superior race and that all brunettes, even Alpines and Mediterraneans of the white race, are a distinctively inferior order of human beings.

Nordicism is a highly contagious disease, and of rather recent origin. In our own history there have been three outbreaks of this epidemic: in the 1850's, the Know-Nothing or American Party; in the 1880's, the American Protective Association; and in the 1920's, a revival of the Ku Klux Klan.

In general the venom of its attack has been against foreigners and in particular against the Catholics, Negroes, and Jews. These outbreaks were the occasion of crimes against both property and person.

Chinese, Japanese, Filipino and Hindu on the Pacific Coast have suffered much at the hands of Nordic mobs.

Friends believe with Paul that "God hath made of one blood all the nations of the earth." This belief causes them to oppose capital punishment for any crime whatsoever, and, of course, they cannot take part in mob violence.

### VIII

Although in the South the Civil War meant the destruction of slavery, in the North it meant the rise of the industrial dinosaurs.

The period following may best be described in the words of Chief Justice Ryan of the Wisconsin Supreme Court who spoke as follows to a commencement class of 1873: "There is looming up a new and dark power. The enterprises of the Country are aggregating vast corporate combinations of unexampled capital, boldly marching, not for economic conquest only, but for political power. For the first time really in our politics, money is taking the field as an organized power. . . . The question will arise, and arise in your day, though perhaps not fully in mine. Which shall rule—wealth or man; which shall lead—money or intellect; who shall fill public stations—educated and patriotic free men, or feudal serfs of corporate capital?"

The philosophy of this period is expressed in the words "business is business," which interpreted means that a business man is rationalizing a shady deal just completed or chloroforming his conscience for one contemplated. There is a companion expression to the effect that business and religion do not mix. This expression interpreted means that the speaker wears the cloak of religion on Sunday and for the rest of the week keeps it in a cellophane wrapper marked with the inscription "not to be opened until next Sunday."

The doctrine of the "Divine Right of Big Business" was never better stated than in a letter of President Baer of the Reading Railway Company to an employee in 1902: ". . . you are evidently biased in favor of the right of the working man to control a business in which he has no other interest than to secure fair wages for the work he does. . . . The rights and interests of the laboring man will be protected and cared for—not by the labor agitator, but by the Christian men to whom God in His infinite wisdom has given the control of the property interests of the country. . . ." Can our political democracy endure unless there is also industrial democracy?

## IX

Ours is a dynamic society. A series of inventions and discoveries have made many rather rapid changes in our methods of production, transportation, communication, and the ways of living and doing things in general. Material traits change more rapidly than non-material. Things change faster than ideas. The resulting strains and stresses often cause crime.

When the American pioneers crossed the Alleghany mountains and homesteaded one hundred and sixty acres each they tried a way of living that had never been tried in the world before. The smallest social and political unit before that time had been the small village. The single family living on an isolated farm acquired valuable traits of initiative, independence, and self-reliance, but they failed to learn the equally valuable traits of cooperation and social responsibility which are necessary when people live in cities. As a result when urbanization came on a large scale the American people had no tradition of communal life and the art of living together; consequently our cities have been centers of crime.

Cultural lags and the complexities of city life have disastrously affected the American home. It has lost many of its economic, educational, and social functions. The children spend their time in school, at the movies, or on the streets. The father and mother frequently are away much of the time on business or pleasure. Juvenile delinquency is the result.

The increase in the number of the socially inadequate, the insane, the feeble-minded, drug addicts, and alcoholics, is alarming. This factor of crime has come upon us so swiftly and stealthily that we do not yet realize its seriousness.

It is difficult to appraise the influence that legal technicalities and delays have upon the rate of crime. But the great majority of the American people are convinced that the peculiarities of the legal code and court procedure encourage criminals to believe that they can commit crime with relative impunity. This does not mean that the legal profession furnishes the motive for crime but it does make the occasion of it easier.

According to Hoffman the three outstanding crime factors in the United States are: first, carrying concealed weapons, "gun-toting" in the South; second, the wide distribution of crime literature; third, long-drawn-out criminal trials.

Inadequate pay and training, third degree methods, political pressure on one hand and public demand for conviction on the other, cause the police as a whole to be both the cause and the occasion of much violation of law.

## X. SUMMARY AND CONCLUSION

An unsatisfactory social, political, religious, and economic status in Europe impelled restless and oppressed peasants and lower middle classes to seek a better home in the New World.

They were actuated by four guiding principles: a political philosophy that stressed the rights of man but not his duties; a theological creed that emphasized the moral efficacy of work and wealth; the immorality of play and pleasure; and the belief in the superiority of the white race and the consequent inferiority of all other races.

When such a heterogeneous people with such ideas were transplanted three thousand miles across the ocean into a sparsely settled continent of vast natural resources to be exploited, all the signs pointed toward a lawless future.

When home ties were broken and the most law-abiding element was cast out a career of crime was assured.

The industrial revolution with its consequent urbanization and disorganization of the home has further complicated the problem of developing an orderly society.

The average American looks upon his lawless heritage with pride and it must be said that the restless spirit of the pioneer accomplished much that has been good. But the thoughtful American faces the future with serious misgivings. Before the depression had become a tradition every man with thrift and frugality could hope to accumulate a competency for his old age.

But now the demand for old age pensions demonstrates the fallacy of such a hope.

Our traditional philosophy of free competition, rugged individualism, must be replaced by the spirit of co-operation. The highest interests of people, when rightly understood, do not come into conflict.

This doctrine applied to the problem of crime means that our ideas of law enforcement, meeting violence with violence, will not be sufficient. The appeal for law observance is too negative. It does not reach the heart of the trouble.

The only solution to the problem of crime lies in a frank acceptance of the precept of the great Teacher, "Thou shalt love thy neighbor as thyself." That is, we must respect the rights and the personality of all our neighbors and thus by mutuality of exchange, where no injustice and no great inequalities of wealth will tempt one man to turn his hand against another, we will develop a society where in the true sense all men are free and equal.

Relying upon the guidance of that Light that lighteth every man that cometh into the world and trying to love their neighbors as themselves, Friends have always endeavored to live in the spirit of peace which takes away all occasion for strife, internal and external.

# XII

## THE PROBLEM OF PEACE

### Frederick J. Libby, S.T.B.

Secretary, National Council for the Prevention of War

CAN we hope for genuine peace in a period of conflict and instability like this? A worldwide struggle between fascist and communist ideologies threatens democracy. The nations are preparing competitively for war. The industrial field, like the international field, is torn with strife. In 1936 more than two thousand strikes were declared in our country; and in the month of March, 1937, six hundred and ten. In our home life there is much misunderstanding between youth and age, while the number of our divorces should make us thoughtful.

Peace may be called the art of living happily together. It is evident that we are far from mastering this art. Science has dissected the atom and can measure the distance of the stars but has not yet taught us how we are to live peaceably with all our neighbors. When a situation of bitter conflict arises between groups or nations or races, which of us is competent to solve the difficulty and achieve peace? To our shame be it said, the Church has thus far usually divided like the unchurched when conflict has arisen and has supplied far too few "peacemakers." Can Friends help a baffled world to find the way to peace, not at some future time, but now?

We shall have to begin by ridding our minds, and ridding the world, of the notion that peace means the preservation of the *status quo*. This is an age-old fallacy that has caused much trouble throughout history. Peace to many of us suggests a placid lake on a summer afternoon. Prophets and other agitators have always been treated as disturbers of the peace.

The plain fact is that there is no *status quo* to be disturbed. John Foster Dulles, in a brilliant address on the subject, "Peaceful Change Within the Society of Nations," delivered at Princeton University March 19, 1936, built his case upon this foundation:

"We are becoming increasingly aware of the dynamic character of the world in which we live. Formerly a large part of what surrounds us was classed as 'solid' and 'static.' Step by step, as our knowledge has progressed, we have had to discard such views. We now know that everything is in motion and that, if there is any one principle of general applicability, it is that of movement and of change. We still speak, to be sure, of the 'static' and the 'maintenance of the *status quo*,' just as we still speak of the 'rising' and the 'setting' of the sun. But such phrases are no longer looked upon as expressing scientific truth. Actually nothing is static; change is omnipresent and the *status quo* is never maintained."

Not only is change the most widely applicable law of Nature but it is also, as Mr. Dulles goes on to say, the only constant factor in human relations. Why should one be surprised that misunderstandings arise between two vital human beings—a father and his growing son, for example—when they spend most of their waking hours in different circles, different occupations, different environments? Change is the universal law. Our Creator is a living God; and life is change. They waste their strength who try to prevent it, for they are fighting the universe.

This brings us to our second observation and to the heart of our subject. Since we must accept change as inevitable, our choice is only between violent change and peaceful change. Peace is not to be identified with stagnation but with peaceful change. "If we desire to avoid impetuous floods," says Mr. Dulles in the address already referred to, "we canalize the stream and diffuse the water at an early stage. By careful planning we can impart to change an element of selectivity. Thus we attain what we are pleased to call 'progress' as distinct from pure 'change.'" Let us see how helpful this analogy can be.

Start with the home. A true living peace in the home is a rarer achievement than may be supposed. It cannot be attained by the exertion of parental authority for that would bring merely stagnation produced by damming forces that are bound to find an outlet. Nor is peace between any two persons a mechanical arrangement to be committed to parchment and packed away. It is an organic relationship, changing with every thought and emotion; a fellowship so intimate that understanding bridges the differences occasioned by the differing environments and mutual affection heals the constantly recurring wounds. Being a spiritual relationship, it is best understood in the light of one's peace with God, the Spirit whom we can approach only when our hearts are right towards those about us.

Turning next to the industrial field and accepting again the inevitability of change, we find ourselves confronted with the same choice: shall change be violent or peaceful? Even the most superficial observation of the facts that surround us bears out the accuracy of the analogy. Dam the dynamic forces that are manifest in the labor movement and violence follows; on the other hand, co-operative planning prevents violence. To those who are seeking light on the "canalization" of the powerful forces that are pressing for industrial democracy, we suggest study of a classic declaration of principles, attributed to Edward Costigan and written, so it is understood, at the request of Josephine Roche, which will be found as the preface to an agreement between the Northern Colorado Coal Producers Association and the United Mine Workers of America. We reproduce it here in full:

### "DECLARATION OF PRINCIPLES

"We, the signers of this document, seeking a new era in the industrial relations of Colorado, unite in welcoming this opportunity to record the spirit and principles of this Agreement.

"Our purposes are:

"To promote and establish industrial justice;

"To substitute reason for violence, confidence for misunderstanding, integrity and good faith for dishonest practices, and a union of effort for the chaos of the present economic warfare;

"To avoid needless and wasteful strikes and lockouts through the investigation and correction of their underlying causes;

"To establish genuine collective bargaining between mine workers and operators through free and independent organization;

"To stabilize employment, production, and markets through co-operative endeavor and the aid of science, recognizing the principle that increased productivity should be mutually shared through the application of equitable considerations to the rights of workers and to economic conditions affecting the operations and business of the company;

"To assure mine workers and operators continuing mutual benefits and consumers a dependable supply of coal at reasonable and uniform prices;

"To defend our joint undertaking against every conspiracy or vicious practice which seeks to destroy it; and in all other respects to enlist public confidence and support by safeguarding the public interest

It is in the field of international relations that we have seen the most graphic examples of the effect of trying to perpetuate a status quo. The Versailles Treaty was such an attempt. The historical map of Europe pictures the failure of every such effort. President Wilson, in his Fourteen Points, proposed a flexible economic and political world system culminating in a League of Nations that would diffuse the dangerous forces that gather around national boundaries before they burst these barriers. His program was not carried out and Article Nineteen of the Covenant, on which the success of his plan partly depended, was made a dead letter by the World War victors. The result is the present armament race with grave danger of another war.

Peace between nations, like peace in the industrial field and in the home, requires a spirit of friendly co-operation as between "good neighbors." Such a relationship is to the enlightened self-interest of both parties and needs to be recognized as such by a well-informed public opinion. As the "Declaration of Principles" in the coal industry indicates, peace begins with a sincere purpose to establish justice. Sometimes the hope of justice will tide over a long period of injustice but this hope is indispensable. The rearmament of the "Haves," if designed merely to maintain by force their privileges, can bring no peace to the world. Like all other efforts to dam up the world's dynamic forces, it can only serve to increase the awfulness of the devastation when it comes. The desperate efforts which the "Have-nots" have been making to increase their bargaining power at the conference table will not be brought to an end by mere frustration of their purpose, leading to another dictated peace. Adjustments and readjustments are going to be necessary. Treaties should for a while be easily terminable at the will of either party. The present distribution of the earth's resources among the races and among the nations is so unjust that it cries to high heaven. A period of change lies before us. It is for present possessors of the earth's resources to make this period one of peaceful change.

When we consider by what methods we are going to achieve a higher degree of justice and cooperation in our various relationships, we find a developing technique already at hand. The conference table, while not always peaceful in its spirit, is nevertheless the very heart of peaceful procedure. The foreign minister of one of the smaller European nations expressed regret when it was proposed to reduce the number of sessions of the Council of the League of Nations because, he said, for several weeks before and after each of those meetings the foreign secretary of a rival state ceased to annoy him. While mere propinquity in itself is not necessarily conducive to peace and may promote irritation and estrangement, nevertheless, when sincere men and women meet to discuss questions of vital interest under the watchful eye of society, itself always an interested party to such a conference, experience shows that progress is likely to be made.

This is not the place to go into an extended discussion of the variety of methods now available for the peaceful settlement of differences. Sometimes the good offices of a third party are sought by the contestants. Sometimes cases are settled "out of court" by the process known as conciliation, each side making concessions. Sometimes disputes are carried through the courts until a decision is reached which neither litigant is then free to question. The process known as arbitration is of this character, the decisions reached by a court of arbitration being final. Sometimes commissions are appointed to deal with a specific question, comprising representatives of all interested parties. Sometimes standing commissions are set up to deal with certain types of disputes. Just as a well-equipped workshop will contain tools adapted exactly to different uses, so the seeker after peace has at hand today all of the tools he requires.

Yes, we know now the ways to peace. We have the tools. Who will use them? Who can use them? In the period of far-reaching change that faces us in the industrial world, who are the men so just, so full of understanding, so highly trusted, that they will be natural and successful arbiters in what will often be a bitter fight? Who are the employers, the workmen, whose foresight and excellent spirit will prevent the "damming up of dynamic forces" and consequent strikes? Who are the teachers that will inculcate in their students the necessity of early mastery of these ways of promoting peace? Who are the leaders of public opinion, the statesmen, the editors, the writers, the holders of public office, that will guide the peoples of the world to peaceful solutions of their problems?

We need peacemakers. We have never realized before how we need them. Our civilization will perish if we pursue further the ways of violence. The time has come when we must learn how to live happily and peacefully with *all* our neighbors. This means that we should from childhood learn how to apply the principles of peaceful change.

Peace is not just a question of method, however. Peace is a way of life. Peace is truly "indivisible." We are going to learn in a deeper sense than we have hitherto experienced the truth of the Beatitude: "Blessed are the peacemakers: for they shall be called the children of God."

# XIII

## Quakerism Through Oriental Eyes

*Takeo Iwahashi*

Kwansai University, Kobe, and Principal of the Toei Girls' English
Institute, Osaka

### FRIENDS

And ye who bear the precious name of Friends,
Boast not to see the Master's whole design,
Who would be wise may wisdom's claim resign,
So far God's plan our simple wit transcends.
No cumbrous load the gospel yoke subtends,
Of many branches is the heavenly vine,
Who tastes God's love is careless to define,
A little child looks up and comprehends.
From self-indulgence keep your thought unstained,
As trusted stewards observe your Master's will,
Judge no man but by wisdom from above.
In every nerve be honesty engrained,
So shall ye have your maiden virtue still
As heaven enfolds the earth in arms of love.
                                        —*William Bacon Evans.*

THE realist is one who sees things as they are and is satisfied. The materialist is one who reduces life to matter and activity, and considers that sufficient. The idealist wanders about in a world of ideas, and is apt to forget the actuality under his feet. The mystic is the only one who, while holding to the actual, has a mystical power that changes the actual into the potential world. Instead of reasoned speech he persists in the eloquence of silence in a world of human conduct.

293

The gospel of John reveals that that which was in the beginning was the Logos. It was word, and at the same time it was deed. The true Christian is he who puts into modern life the word and the deed of God. But in order to be a true Christian, it is necessary, while holding to the actual, to transcend it, and to change the super-actual into the actual. I do not hesitate to call this twentieth century mystic, a Quaker. Before he can be "a publisher of truth," he must himself grasp the truth. But to grasp truth is nothing other than to experience the living word and deed—in other words, the Logos in action. This is the experience which Paul says is "written not with ink, but with the Spirit of the living God; not in tables of stone, but in fleshly tables of the heart."

It is natural that the truth of the Inner Light should be the ever old yet always new theme of religion. Therefore Quaker principles are not of a nature that can exist in England only, or be permitted holy birth in the United States of North America alone. It must be an experience, a life, which may spring forth in any place on earth where man is. In other words, just as the true gospel and endless life of Christianity consist in making our religion the religion which was in Christ, rather than in making a religion of Christ, so in Quaker principle also, while we accept as fact the things that the early Quaker believed and lived, we must ourselves discover them afresh in the life of today. Therefore in the pure religious or rather Quaker principle, there is neither East nor West.

When a river which has been flowing on the surface sinks under the surface as the result of certain conditions, it reveals a lack of understanding to say that the river no longer exists. For such a subterranean river may again rise to the surface. As one who believes that the current of the life of the universe is a river, I desire from a full heart to urge those pilgrims who are traveling along the banks of that river of life not to fall into this illusion or error. In my own experience, after encountering life's catastrophe in the loss of my eyesight, at the moment when I thought all things had turned to ashes, I was blessed with the experience of entering "the narrow gate" that leads from darkness into light. When I consider this sacred experience, it is as if the river of life which at one time had sunk from sight had again gushed forth before my eyes. In truth, it must be said, God is love, and because He is love, when He closes a door before us He opens a window in its stead. As a result of this proof by experience, I cannot but be deeply impressed by the fact that Quakerism is one of the mystical powers which is always at our call.

Just as in an autumn garden chrysanthemums (the Orient) and dahlias (the Occident) compete side by side in beauty, or again as the oil paintings of Millet or Cézanne may be hung on the wall of a severely simple Japanese guestroom alcove

without losing a sense of harmony, so the mystic
of the Orient and of the Occident, each with his
own characteristics, may incarnate his words in
deeds. Concealed in the differing forms and expressions lie deeper meanings and values. When
we think of this as the "Inner Light," not separated
from life, we understand that this universal and
holy thing which transcends time and space is the
love in God, is truth. For this reason the Quaker
is to be found not only in the past of the Orient,
but in the present and may be expected in the future. It may be he does not himself realize that
he is a Quaker, but if in reality he be one, will not
his discovery be a beautiful experience? For in
this world the true mystic does not testify to his
own mysticism. If we think that when his name
is written in the heavenly book of life man becomes a true Christian, then it is clear we shall
have to discount much of that type of Christian
who beats his own drums before his face. Are
not these unreal professions of Christianity evident when we look at the present day tragedy in
which anti-Christian conduct and even crimes are
repeatedly committed in nominally Christian countries? The essential thing is not what appears on
the surface, but the steady even though imperfect
movement towards realization. Whether it be a
matter of the individual or of the group, he who
preaches ideals while idly criticizing the actual
is facing spiritual bankruptcy. The present world
crisis is not limited to the shores of the Atlantic;

it has already crossed the Pacific and has come not alone to China, and not alone to Japan. This situation is demanding great resolution, in face of the inescapable task.

This brings us to the world of those who, having not, suffer, and the world of those who have and yet suffer. Whether it be the power of money, the power of government, of knowledge or of the sword, the swing of the pendulum is ever back and forth between those who have and those who have not. In the recent past the aim of the proletariat was the severe criticism and condemnation of capitalism, but today the concrete movements for its liberation are watched with vigilant eyes. Whether in the form of socialism or of fascism, whenever these work through violent revolution, on the left hand or on the right, strict control has now been established. Whatever be the condition in other countries, in Japan there is light on the problem of controlling violence.

With this necessary social evolution, the privileged classes have been compelled to share with increasing momentum the sufferings of the underprivileged. Today no man can escape this suffering. In the just and equal sharing of this suffering by all classes lies the solution of the unprecedented suffering prevailing since the World War. It is natural that the speed-measure of the movements for alleviation should be the length and cruelty of the centuries through which these sufferings have been endured. Of course the money

297

barons and the political party leaders have felt the new power of these social movements. But not these classes alone, for since the events of May 15, 1932, and of February 26, 1936, even the militarists, which in Japan have held a special place among the privileged classes, have felt the sufferings of those who have and of those who have not.

Facing these facts it is necessary to re-examine the problems of the individual and of society, of the nation and of the world. Herein lies the reason for applying to the Far Eastern situation the meaning and the value of Quakerism.

Believing that the material alone cannot solve the problems of the material and that spirit alone cannot solve the problems of the spirit, I hear the material and the spiritual calling for "Man" as the common meeting place of the material and the spiritual. When we consider the modern problem of science we see that science in itself is neither the friend nor the enemy of culture; it depends upon the way science is used—upon the degree to which the human element enters into the use of science.

The question given at the very end of Wells' "The Shape of Things to Come," viz., "Which shall be chosen?" should have been asked and adequately answered in the very beginning. Even though science succeeds in solving the mysterious laws of the starry heavens, in separating individual atoms into electrons and by radio-activity further divides electrons, and even though it successfully demonstrates the theory of thermo-dynamics, science still remains science. It is utterly unable to decide whether I should eat the piece of bread which lies in my hand or give it to another. In this limitation of science lies the special nature of the present-day world-wide suffering.

So long as we are dealing with life, namely, so long as man remains man, science should remain science, and not seek to dominate life. The control of science cannot be found in science itself. In other words, science is a means for the realization of human values and ideals. Hence it is important to re-examine the limitations in the effectiveness and use of science. Is it not like "fire" in the English proverb: "Fire is a good servant but a bad master"?

Recent Russian materialists have beaten Tolstoi, the star of humanity, to the ground, saying, "He is empty and void of content." But in Tolstoi, who analyzed nineteenth century European civilization with penetrating criticism, and in Schweitzer, whose lancet is dissecting twentieth century culture—in both of these we discern the human elements necessary for the control of science. Kropotkin, who called Tolstoi "the conscience of the nineteenth century," also challenged sharp attention to the essential human element, as when he gave the following warning to Russian rural workers: "My fellow farmers: As you work in the fields, do not be wholly absorbed in the number and size of your potatoes. You must not forget to sing the praises of the dream-like Aurora Borealis which shines over your heads."

One can say the same thing concerning religion. Some of our established religious organizations are today being assailed by fierce storms of police inquiry. This does not mean that religion itself is bad; it depends upon the interpretation of the nature of religion, from which evils may spring. The same thing may also be said of government and of education. One can also recognize this same need for intensive self-criticism in the ideology of labor, which has come to count itself all but infallible.

I do not hesitate to approve the present movement which seeks through changes in social policy, without revolution, the gradual reform of capitalism, with security and enlarged life for the people. But I do not believe this movement will immediately give us an ideal society, for it is a method which does not hold in itself the elements of an ideal society. It is like the violent revolutions springing from Bolshevism and other swift movements for equality, which certainly will not reach the desired goal.

So long as men seek to interpret material things by material things and to solve the problem of movements by other movements, the only abiding results will be material things and movements—not the object sought. Granted the attainment of the goal, if the method used be merely a "method," without the elements of the ideals sought, the new society created will be only one of method or means. If a great ideal society be the goal, the means used must contain in themselves the elements of the desired ideal society.

In the same way, if the goal of medical science be the conquering of all disease, the highest ideal must be for all doctors to lose their jobs. This means that when the method dies the true object is born. It is like the caterpillar turning into the chrysalis and the chrysalis into the butterfly. We must therefore recognize that so long as a social policy remains as a social policy, that is, so long as the authoritative attitude toward social problems remains unchanged and limited the goal attained will inevitably be limited.

It is thus seen that in dealing with the material, the spiritual element is necessary, and when dealing with the spiritual, material things are necessary. We must recognize that the means employed and the object sought are inseparable. As we carefully examine this law, we must discern the necessity for a "working place" where the "Holy Experiment" of introducing the human element can take place. In other words, in dealing with every problem we return to mystical "man." Therefore in dealing with all problems of government, economics, science, arts, social policies, social legislation and social work, the key which can unlock them all is not found in policies, ideologies, movements and works, but in man who carries on these movements and these works and who is affected by them. In short, the key lies, both static and dynamic, in the means used. The reason for this is that since both those who have and those who have not are today suffering together, the essential thing is a view of human life and a universal faith which depend neither upon possession nor upon non-possession.

In his book *The Power of Non-Violence,* Richard B. Gregg carefully examines and applies to political, economic, social and industrial problems the power of non-violence (spiritual resistance), which was first emphasized by Tolstoi and which is now being perfected by Mahatma Gandhi. This is a living book, challenging the attention with the authority of the spirit to a share in the solution of material problems.

In this connection it is fitting to consider the experiment being carried on at the "Ittoen" (Single-Light-Garden) in the suburbs of Kyoto, in which the Order of Francis of Assisi has become "Japanized." This movement is embodying in practical life the wide-spread but unrealized teachings of Tolstoi. Here is being created a holy laboratory where a vigorous peace order is living the simple life of love, service and voluntary poverty.

When a man stands penniless on the street two possible roads lie before him. He may proceed with passionate revolutionary songs and bombs or he may begin a life of penitence and service. Can we not say that this moment of decision is the watershed of human life? The first course deals with things and hence may appear to be positive, but in reality it is not. The latter course proceeds from within and hence, though it appears to be negative, is in reality positive. Is it better to suffer defeat through victory or to win victory through defeat? The kind of non-resistance which is prepared for defeat is not power, but that which suffers defeat in order to win is the way to power.

When I am to decide whether I should eat the piece of bread in my hand or give it to another I find science and the world of things quite impotent in themselves to give me any light. At such a moment the value of what I have called the "human element" comes to our aid as a guiding principle. And herein lies the twentieth century glory of the cross of the penniless Christ, who will not find in Karl Marx an enemy, but a good servant. Here lies also the meaning of the life of Tenko Nishida, founder of the "Ittoen" of Kyoto, who does not place wholesale condemnation upon Lenin, but by the prayer of his life calmly points to the seat of power.

In this dying to mere personal desires and self-interest we clearly discover the true laws of social life, which consist in self-denial and the spirit of service. All social policies which aim only at giving protection through material help and relief through protection (important and necessary as these are) tend merely to postpone the day of ultimate solutions.

The beginning of the real solution of social problems is discovered in the creation of a spirit in which a man finds an inward drive to rise penniless, even though he receives no outside protection and no help. In other words, the first step toward the solution of the problem lies in first giving as leaven what comes at the end. It is the human element, where the material and spiritual worlds combine and blend in harmony, which alone can form the abiding foundation for the realization of genuine, creative social policies, social legislation and social work. This is the reason for the true saying of Turgeniev that the first spade must be struck deeply into the virgin soil. The only effective principle for restoring true peace and happiness to the present generation, suffering in chaotic confusion, material and spiritual, requires nothing less than the courageous seeking of life through death. The desired social ideals can be realized only in a world where social policies and social work die in ceasing to serve merely as means to attain the ultimate ideals. Here lies the necessity for the human element to vitalize all social policies.

This kind of a spirit must of necessity respond to the material world. At the same time this material world is essential to spiritual understanding. When the vertical spiritual law running through our spirits, our bodies and our whole life unites with the horizontal social law running through our living, our homes and our social organizations, thus creating a clear consciousness of man's inherent personal and social values, and when spiritual and social laws are no longer held as mere ideals but are embodied in practice, then we may expect release from the prevailing world suffering.

Venturing to designate this as the Oriental point of view, I wish to submit it as a suggestion toward the solution of the problems of world suffering which seem to baffle Western social theories. For here lies the gospel of non-possession and the philosophy of life through death. This philosophy, as it is being demonstrated in the lives of two great Orientals, Mahatma Gandhi and Tenko Nishida, will strengthen our wills for the simple life and for truth, giving us the unswerving life-courage to surmount the surging waves of human desires and consumption economy. In the terms of fractions, these Oriental mystics take "one" as the numerator and place it over "zero," which equals "nothing," but they seek through this "nothingness," as their "Logos," to realize the unified experience of word and deed.

The Oriental contribution to Quakerism must be the mysticism contained in the principle of "nothingness." Bubbles floating on the surface of the Pacific Ocean never reach shore so long as they remain bubbles. But when they die and sink into the waters of the Ocean, the fragile bubbles instantly embrace both shores of the Pacific. In this way both the East and the West need to return to

God, and by returning to God the realization of higher world ideals will become possible.

This humble chapter in this memorable book is dedicated with the desire that what I have tried to explain may become one of the corner stones of this emerging world. "If these should hold their peace the stones would immediately cry out." While listening to these crying stones, the Oriental mystics, though the form and method of expression be different, join with Western mystics and, guided by the same life and light, seek through the subterranean currents to realize in daily life the truth that faith and life are one. These Oriental mystics have laid hold upon the world of love and peace lying beyond darkness and confusion.

THE END